Bowery Mission

Bowery Mission

Grit and Grace
on Manhattan's
Oldest Street

Jason Storbakken

PLOUGH PUBLISHING HOUSE

Published by Plough Publishing House
Walden, New York, USA
Robertsbridge, England, UK
Elsmore, NSW, Australia
www.plough.com

ISBN: 978-0-87486-254-6
22 21 20 19   1 2 3 4 5 6

A catalog record for this book is available from the British Library.

Library of Congress Cataloging-in-Publication Data

Names: Storbakken, Jason, author.
Title: Bowery mission : grit and grace on Manhattan's oldest street / Jason
  Storbakken.
Description: Walden : Plough Publishing House, 2019. | Summary: "A colorful
  history of lives rescued on New York City's infamous boulevard of broken
  dreams. The Bowery has long been one of New York City's most notorious
  streets, a magnet for gangsters, hucksters, and hobos. And despite
  sweeping changes, it is still all too often the end of the road for
  troubled war veterans, drug addicts, the mentally ill, the formerly
  incarcerated, and others generally down on their luck. Against this
  backdrop, for 140 years, Christians of every stripe have been coming
  together at the Bowery Mission to offer hearty meals, hot showers, clean
  beds, warm clothes - and, for thousands of homeless over the years, the
  help they need to get off the streets and back on their feet. Jason
  Storbakken, a recent Bowery director, retraces that colorful history and
  profiles some of the illustrious characters that have made the Bowery an
  iconic New York institution. His book offers a lens through which to
  better understand the changing faces of homelessness, of American
  Christianity, and of New York City itself - all of which converge daily
  at the Bowery Mission's red doors"-- Provided by publisher.
Identifiers: LCCN 2019024761 (print) | LCCN 2019024762 (ebook) | ISBN
  9780874862546 (hardcover) | ISBN 9780874862553 (epub) | ISBN
  9780874862553 (mobi)
Subjects: LCSH: Bowery Mission and Young Men's Home (New York, N.Y.) |
  Rescue missions (Church work)--New York (State)--New York.
Classification: LCC BV2656.N4 B677 2020 (print) | LCC BV2656.N4 (ebook) |
  DDC 267/.13097471--dc23
LC record available at https://lccn.loc.gov/2019024761
LC ebook record available at https://lccn.loc.gov/2019024762

Printed in the United States

To my mother, Tammy Wolf, who has shown me what it means to care for the most vulnerable, even at great personal cost. And to my father, Mark Tschetter, who always told me to "look out for the little guys."

Table of Contents

Foreword

have always felt that the ultimate spiritual deception
we can experience as believers in Jesus is to empha-
size our relationship with God, with little concern
for the less fortunate around us. That was exactly the
problem in ancient Israel when the prophet Isaiah lifted
his voice on behalf of the living God:

> They come to the Temple every day and seem delighted
> to learn all about me. . . . They ask me to take action
> on their behalf pretending they want to be near me.
> "We have fasted before!" they say. "Why aren't you
> impressed?" . . . No, this is the kind of fasting I want:
> Share your food with the hungry and give shelter to the
> homeless. Give clothes to those that need them. . . . Feed
> the hungry and help those in trouble. Then your light
> will shine out from the darkness. . . . You will be like
> a well-watered garden, like an ever-flowing spring."
> (Isaiah 58, NLT)

Those words have challenged me throughout the years I have pastored in the inner city of downtown Brooklyn. But it hasn't always been easy to put them into practice.

One Sunday years ago, after I ended a service, I looked up and there was a guy standing in the aisle about four rows back with a filthy cap in his hand, his hands crossed in front of him, just looking at me. At the time, we had a lot of people coming in begging for money. Like many churches, we had a protocol for how to help them.

This guy looks like he wants to talk to me, so I say, "Come on up." When he gets close to me, I'm hit with the worst smell – feces, urine, sweat, street – overwhelming to the point that it seems to me I cannot inhale facing him. So I look to the side and say, "What's your name?"

"David."

"Where'd you sleep last night?"

"Abandoned truck."

"Why aren't you in the shelter?"

"Too dangerous, almost got killed in the last one." There is alcohol on his breath, and his eyes are slightly glazed. I look around, but there's nobody to help me. I'm tired, so I think: forget the protocol, let me just give him some money, I gotta get home. He steps forward, pushes the money down, and says, "I don't want your money. I want this Jesus you were just talking about."

I say, "Take the money."

He says, "No, I don't want your money. I'm going to die out there. I want Jesus."

At that moment I realized the one who was really in need was not David, it was Jim Cymbala. I stood there and started weeping and praying, "God, would you please forgive me. I have turned into my own worst nightmare. I have become what I dread thinking about: a preacher." I had been in and around church since I was a kid, so that was my ultimate nightmare, some phony guy who just talks: "Well Praise God, JC's in the house." I had become that. I wanted to buy him off, because I was tired.

As God began to break me and fill me with his love, David knew it in a second. He knew it and came close to me; he fell against me, put his head on my chest, and started crying. I put my arms around him and he put his arms around me, and we rocked back and forth. I'm crying because I need Jesus, he's crying because he needs Jesus. We all need Jesus. And I felt the Lord speak to me and say, "If you can't embrace that smell, I can't use you, because the whole world smells like that to me and I still sent my son. So if you can't accommodate yourself to that smell and embrace it, I'll put you on a shelf. I don't need to use you. I can use anybody. I'm God."

There are people who are very hard to be around. If you don't want to be around not-nice people, you need to resign from following Jesus. Jesus didn't come for nice people, he came for the whole world and we're all in need of him. The Bowery Mission has been blessed with a special kind of love that allows for transformative relationships between not-nice people. The Bowery Mission shows this love every day – and joining with them in this love, in this mission, is exactly what God has called us to do.

An associate pastor recently asked me if we could hold a wedding ceremony for a couple who wanted to get married but were impoverished. I agreed. The day before the event I learned that not only was the groom living in a shelter but they had no money for the bride's corsage or a wedding cake. Less than an hour before the service began, I met the groom for the first time and asked him about the exchange of rings. He sheepishly looked down at the floor and confessed they had no rings due to a lack of funds.

But despite all of that, what followed was a night to remember! The audience cheered when I announced the surprise wedding and they showered the couple with love all the way through the ceremony. I was deeply moved as the two of them stood before me, so poor by worldly standards, yet so rich spiritually in Jesus and now part of a huge family that embraced them. Multiply that story by the thousands, and you will get an idea of the impact of the Bowery Mission.

Bowery Mission: Grit and Grace on Manhattan's Oldest Street recounts the original vision and ongoing saga of the Bowery Mission as it continues to help the neediest among us on the streets of New York City. Jason

Storbakken has written with skill and transparency as he relates one poignant story after another. Read this with an open heart to God and a readiness to do your part in showing the love of Jesus to the world around you.

Pastor Jim Cymbala
Brooklyn Tabernacle
April 2019

1 Welcome to the Bowery

The muffled hum of morning traffic gets louder and more distinct as I climb the stairs from the subway. Sirens wail, and I hear a truck's angry blare – some urgent food delivery no doubt – above engine thrum and radio thump and throb. As I emerge, exhaust fumes swirl away the stairwell's stagnant air, and I quickly scan Bowery and Houston Streets. When I first came here, I did this to orient myself, having lost all sense of direction in the sub-city tangle. Nearly ten years on, I know this neighborhood like the back of my hand, yet I still glance around reflexively as soon as I arrive – scanning for trouble as well as friendly faces. Vehicles and pedestrians pour past, as Houston is one of the main arteries into Lower Manhattan.

Before turning the corner onto the Bowery, I stop to converse with Shirley. In her wheelchair beside a spattered wall, she is begging spare change, as usual. She's in her fifties. Burn scars mar her face, neck, and arms, and she is missing a leg and several fingers. Shirley told me her story several years ago. Her childhood and adolescence were nothing unusual, she said. Content within her intersecting circles of family and friends, she never felt afraid or insecure. But one day when she was eighteen, someone forced her into a car, raped her, held a lighter to her clothes, and threw her out of the vehicle. She did not tell me if the perpetrator was a stranger or someone she knew.

Shirley's psychological injuries were even worse than the physical ones, and she has spent most of her life on the streets or in and out of hospitals, mental health facilities, and shelters. At times, she emits gut-wrenching wails or rants incoherently – and passersby avert their eyes and quicken their steps. If I pause to say, "Hi Shirley!" during one of these frantic episodes, she'll calm down to respond, "Well hello, Pastor Jason," becoming lucid through being recognized and named. Authentic relationship and human connection has incredible power to transform.

Turning right, I walk south, past bottle shops, pop-up tattoo parlors, and graffiti-splashed storefronts. Many establishments have signs in Chinese as well as English; we're not far from Chinatown. I pass some high-end new developments, shoehorned between crumbling façades. Progress is pressing its way onto the mile-and-a-half-long Bowery, but the squalid conditions that gave Manhattan's oldest street[1] its reputation still surround me.

Navigating around broken paving slabs, a fire barrel, lumpy garbage bags – familiar hazards – I'm more concerned about tripping on human beings. There are still a few on the sidewalk at nine o'clock, stoned or sleeping. I know some by name, and I might come back in an hour or two to chat or bring them coffee. They know they are welcome at the Mission. They also know I respect their choice when they stay away.

Outside a place advertising restaurant equipment, two guys are hosing down a used meat slicer. I sidestep into the street to avoid being sprayed. The shouted conversation is pidgin English or perhaps Creole. Meanwhile, a layer of fat is forming on the wet curb, and iridescent pigeons pick through greasy runoff oozing toward the nearest drain.

After passing a couple more kitchen appliance stores, I can see my goal behind scaffolding uprights: the crimson doors of the Bowery Mission. The walk from the subway has taken barely five minutes. But now an old friend, Red, steps into my path, signaling me to stop – as predictable as the pigeons. Everyone on the Bowery knows this elderly gentleman, both because he hauls cardboard from the local businesses and because he shares his limitless fund of wisecracks with almost anyone he meets, choosing the joke to fit the person. Red and I are still chuckling over his latest when three women in fashionable attire and tinted glasses swish past, heading toward New Museum – which towers over the Mission and brings a steady flow of tourists to our corner of the Lower East Side.

A few more strides, and I've arrived. Kimbell Frazer greets me at the door. He runs the front desk and provides a warm welcome to all who enter – staff, guest, or volunteer.

During my years at the Bowery Mission, I have immersed myself in this street's rich history and culture. On good days, I sense God's presence here – in the folk I encounter and even in our chapel's odor. The stink used to repulse me, especially in summertime heat, until a thought grabbed me: the chapel walls and pews absorb the smell of the homeless as Christ's cross absorbs the world's sin. From that day, the reek of sweat and urine became *almost* aromatic. In this place, I have heard the hopes and hardships of hundreds or perhaps even thousands.

Jerry has Tourette syndrome, with violent muscle spasms. His manic energy prevents him sitting long during chapel, and I have to remind him to watch his language when he eats in Fellowship Hall. Once he was jailed for months after accidentally knocking someone out with a compulsive spasm. But authorities never addressed his neurological disorder.

Cowboy, another Bowery associate, disappeared for a couple of years. Everyone assumed he had drunk himself to death, until he stumbled back one day. His physical and mental condition had so deteriorated, however, that his return seemed less like a resurrection than a scene from *The Walking Dead*.

Wheelchair Charlie would catch some sleep on a train or in the park, but police always made him move on. After decades of this and a corresponding decline in his health, his swollen legs had to be amputated, and he eventually died of complications. Too many have died, some of whose names I never even learned. The chief medical examiner will occasionally call me to come and identify a body. I see a lot of death on the Bowery.

Beverly had a stroke and could no longer walk from her apartment to the Mission. Martin beat up Aliya in the Mission lobby. And Bernie beat up Laura. . . .

These are my acquaintances, my flock, my community?

Yes, these are some of the characters who share my life and shape my thinking. Since my 2010 arrival on the Bowery, many of them have accompanied me to schools, churches, and seminaries across the country, to tell what living on the street is like. A number have stayed in my home, spending Christmas with my family.

Homeless people are not the good-for-nothing bums portrayed by the media. Most find themselves on the street through a combination of flawed systems and traumatic personal history. They don't fit into a culture that exalts independence, which too often translates as disconnectedness or just plain loneliness when you have no family or community. Many, like Shirley and Jerry, are incapable of caring for themselves. Others are troubled war veterans. Some were set on their downward course by structural racism. And many struggle with addiction. Society's view of substance abuse as criminal, rather than as a health issue comparable to mental illness, often inhibits them from asking for help.

A disproportionate number of the homeless come from broken homes. Too often connected with abuse, family breakup can leave those involved mired in shame, which prevents them from seeking help and moving toward recovery. Whatever its cause, family collapse leaves lasting scars.

Take Billy, for example. Although he failed his two tries at the Mission's recovery program, he still drops in for a meal or a change of clothes, and he has told me his story, over time. He is the one who helped me understand that, for kids, foster care and institutionalization are forms of homelessness. I have learned that, on average, a child goes through six placements before aging out, sometimes directly to life on the street.[2]

Billy's first five years were normal, he told me, and his family's house was modest but comfortable. Then his world turned upside down: Child Protective Services arrived one morning and removed him from his home. Billy clung so tightly to the stair banister that the social workers had to pry his fingers loose. None of them took time to explain to the child why he was being taken from his parents, whom he never saw again; today, more than forty years later, he still has no clue.

Billy was put in an orphanage and spent his next five years in institutions before an Italian-American couple finally adopted him. They hoped to give him a happy home, but they were aging and ill equipped to care for a traumatized ten-year-old. They returned Billy to Child Services when he was fifteen, and he entered the foster care system. At seventeen, he escaped foster care – and initially avoided homelessness – by joining the navy. He hoped to find stability but wound up instead with an undesirable discharge. Life felt like a series of rejections – by his birth family, by his adoptive parents, by the military. He then wandered the east coast for several years until, after a prison term for forgery, he found himself on the Bowery.

Too many in Billy's situation resign themselves to feeling worthless, believing no one knows or cares whether they live or die. That is why our residential program invites hurting and homeless men and women to "access comprehensive services for physical, emotional, psychological, and spiritual healing – all in the context of a safe, supportive community."[3] The program's name has varied over the years, but its aim remains constant: to help participants progress from isolation or despair to a purpose-filled life.

Some who arrive hunting emergency food or shelter end up staying, becoming part of our team. Al Moyer survived for over a decade by scrounging in dumpsters and garbage cans, before he walked into the Mission one day looking for shelter from the rain. A lifelong New Yorker, his opportunities growing up had been limited by poverty, and he slid into depression. Alcohol did the rest, as he tried to drown his disappointment. Al discovered that he liked the Mission, however, and after sitting through numerous chapel services, he decided to give faith a try. He completed our recovery program, got back on his feet, and was eventually hired as operations manager. He now gives his weekends to host volunteers. But what Al does best is transmit his optimism to new arrivals.

Vinny, too, spent years "living like a dog," as he described it. Only the persistence of volunteers and staff repeatedly bringing him food in the park persuaded him to visit the Bowery Mission. Here he experienced a conversion that changed every aspect of his life. He told novices in later years:

> Before I came here, I was dead. I was running with drugs. Satan had took everything from me for twenty-six years: my dignity, my respect – *everything* – until he had me laying in the street. If you ain't at that bottom, thank God, but that's the bottom I had to be brought to.

When I first came to this place, I didn't care what it was about. My mind was still out there. But Jesus conquered – not with a knife, not with a switchblade, not with a gun – he conquered with *love*.

When I came into this program, I didn't read the Bible as much as people wanted me to. My mind was all banged up. But I read the Gospels. What stuck out to me was: you are forgiven . . . don't let your left hand know what your right is doing . . . visit your brothers in the hospital . . . visit your brothers in prison . . . be careful when you entertain strangers, because some have entertained angels. That came to me when I worked the front desk. So I have to be kind. Not because I want to, but because Jesus commands me to. That's the bottom line.

Vinny eventually became a counselor. "Look at me," he would tell anyone feeling low. "I had no family two years ago. *Nobody* wanted this man! But Jesus did. Sometimes I step back, and it blows me away." Convinced that faith can only survive with support from fellow believers, Vinny made himself a brother to anyone entering the Mission. He challenged Martin, a young volunteer who seemed wavering and directionless, to discover and pursue God's plan for his future – which gave Martin no peace until he did so.

Vinny ultimately died of AIDS, contracted during his former life, yet his joy-filled witness lives on in the countless individuals he touched. And when Martin married and started a family, he and his wife named their first son Vinny.

James Macklin also joined our community from the street. He was born in Virginia in 1939, and his teenage mother put him up for adoption. He was taken into a good home, but his adoptive mother died when he was nine, and he was bumped from one foster home to the next until he found himself on his own at age thirteen. Since early childhood, James had expressed his feelings through song, so he tried to earn a living on the Chitlin Circuit – venues where black entertainers were able to perform during the Jim Crow era. When he couldn't make ends meet, he joined seasonal workers harvesting cotton and tobacco.

James experimented with gambling, alcohol, and marijuana, but it was cocaine that hooked him, and he began hustling to feed his habit. After years of this life-style, he took a job and started saving money, striving to change his ways. When he opened his own office-cleaning business, he believed he had conquered his addictions. Temptation surrounded him, however, and this time crack was his downfall. His business toppled, and by 1987 he was adrift on the streets of New York.

Sleeping on the subway one night, he woke at hearing a woman's voice exclaim, "What's a man like you doing in a place like this?" James opened his eyes to see a white-haired lady holding out a card that offered a meal at the

Bowery Mission. Since he was famished, he took the card and followed its directions.

That was the beginning of his new life. James entered and completed the recovery program and was hired as a Bowery security guard. Three years later, he was promoted to operations manager, and eventually to assistant director. His male choir, "Resurrected Beyond Belief," was one of his greatest contributions to the Bowery Mission. Wherever they performed across the country, James told his listeners what it is like to have no home.

During the 1980s and 90s, the Mission housed a women's program at 227 Bowery. (It later moved to West 15th Street, and there are currently several locations for women in uptown Manhattan.) These women attended the Mission's Sunday service, which is how James Macklin met Debra, who later joined his musical tours. James would sing, and Debra would share her testimony. In 1995 they were wed in the chapel at West 15th Street, and their marriage became a pillar of the Mission. Debra recently retired from her work at the women's center, while James – now in his eighties – continues to sing, welcome newcomers, and host out-of-state volunteers.

During my tenure as Director of Chapel and Compassionate Care, I increasingly came to focus on *care* – and on a similar-sounding Hebrew word, *kara,* "to cry out with" or "to bow down with." Much of my work is simply crying out to God, bowing down in solidarity with those who feel beaten.

Yet as society's outcasts trudge past day after day – odd miscellany spilling from bulging coat pockets, bags, or trundled shopping cart – my compassion sometimes thins and frays. When cursing and fights break out, I can almost feel my heart harden, protecting itself.

Struggling to resist this, I ask myself: Do I truly grasp the humiliation of homelessness? Do I understand our guests' anxiety that transitional housing might lead back to the street – or that a new job may be just one more dead end? How does it feel to know that even hard-fought freedom from addiction can crumble when desperation drives a person to grab the readily available bottle, needle, pipe, or pill?

To remain sensitive, I have learned, I must acknowledge my complicity in the world's problems and my own need for healing. So I don't avoid telling our guests that my mother was an unwed teenager who raised me alone, that I witnessed my share of domestic violence growing up, and that I, too, have served jail time – from a few days in a juvenile facility, at age sixteen, to a three-month stint in a South Korean prison on drug charges. If I make myself vulnerable like this, I can be what Henri Nouwen calls a wounded healer. He writes:

> Through compassion it is possible to recognize that the craving for love that people feel resides also in our own hearts, that the cruelty the world knows all too well is also rooted in our own impulses. Through compassion we also sense our hope for forgiveness in our friends' eyes and our hatred in their bitter mouths. When they kill, we know that we could have done it; when they give life, we know that we can do the same. For a compassionate person nothing human is alien: no joy and no sorrow, no way of living and no way of dying.

My watershed moment came one lunchtime. It was clothing give-out day, and Fellowship Hall was packed with raucous men and women clamoring to get their goods. Suddenly, before my eyes, the place transformed into heaven's great banquet hall. For that infinite second, rude jostlers became God's chosen guests, a forgiving and forgiven people, a loving and beloved community. With this epiphany, I recalled what first brought me here. "You can't lead the people if you don't love the people," Dr. Cornel West used to say, at Union Theological Seminary. "You can't save the people if you don't serve the people."

The vision faded the next instant, and I was back in the dysfunction that every family holds – and perhaps none more than our Bowery family. But conviction and joy had returned, along with confidence that God will keep healing my own wounds and those of my brothers and sisters at the Mission. I was meant to be here, and I am fortunate to witness – and be shaped by – what God is doing in this community.

I see a lot of love and life on the Bowery.

2 Becoming Bowery

A **hundred years before** Billy, Cowboy, and Jerry wandered into the Bowery Mission, John Goode did the same.

Goode grew up in a Colorado mining camp, where his parents ran a boarding house. The silver mine was sixty miles from the nearest railroad, and the boy's mother – "a good woman," he called her – was the only woman in camp. He referred to his father as "a fighting, whiskey-drinking Irishman, as irritable when sober as he was cruel and vicious when drunk."[1] Life was so harsh, three of Goode's younger siblings died within two winters.

At age eleven, to escape his father's anger, Goode ran away from home. He hopped trains and caroused with hobos, stealing and lying his way across the country. He eventually landed in reform school, where he acquired the skills of an astute liar, thief, and gambler. After several years, he graduated from stints in juvenile reformatories to serving time in adult prisons, from San Quentin to the Tombs.

After one jail term, Goode established himself in New York City, doing small jobs for crooks with clout and working his way up from corrupt sanitation worker to corrupt cop. He described his law enforcement career:

> All my life, mind you, I had broken the law – the law of every state and city I'd ever visited. Law was nothing to me. Those who were paid to uphold the law were nothing to me except grafters. . . . Despite my record and my principles, well known to all who were instrumental in securing my appointment, I was made a member of the city police force in June 1900. There, of course, I had all sorts of opportunity for inside information on the ponies. I knew all the poolrooms and all the bookmakers. In addition there were always crooks and gamblers anxious to stand in with the cops and thus I was always getting good tips.[2]

Goode eventually got in so deep that even his cronies couldn't protect him. He had a huge gambling debt and nearly murdered an adversary. One of his many crimes caught up with him, and he did six years' hard labor at Sing Sing.

Released from prison as a defeated man, Goode made his way to the Bowery. There he took a job for which most tramps had too much self-respect: joining the Pinkertons as a strikebreaker. The morning after blowing his first paycheck on booze, he woke in a back alley. "Just as there is but one New York and one Paris and one Venice, so there is but one Bowery," he later said. "Down so low that there's just one of two things left to do – get up or die."[3]

Lying there, Goode thought of his wife, who had
scarcely crossed his mind in years. He had married to get
his hands on Jane's money, and soon after their marriage,
he had gambled it away. She had remained loyal,
however, and in that alley Goode decided to reach out to
the only person who cared about him. When he emerged
and asked where he could get a stamp and stationery, he
was directed to the Bowery Mission. He walked in, for
the first time, to write Jane an apology.

Although he had only come for pen and paper, Goode
was sent to the Mission's Labor Bureau and found
himself employed for the day. Hauling lumber was hard
work and didn't pay well, but it was perhaps the first
honest job he'd ever had. Too exhausted to drink that
night, he got himself a bed in a flophouse. There were
many of these on the Bowery (the term originated as
hobo jargon for the cheapest place to sleep). Next day he
returned to work and began attending evening chapel.[4]
Goode soon took a job at the Mission, and his wife
joined him. He spent his remaining years being the best
husband he could and sharing his redemptive story with
newcomers on the Bowery.[5]

Ever since the Civil War, individuals such as John
Goode – trapped in addiction or mental illness, or
just down on their luck – have found their way to
the Manhattan crossroads of Houston and Bowery.
(Some historians think the word "hobo" comes from a

combination of these streets' names.) When I started
work here, I was curious. How did the Bowery become a
magnet for gangsters and hucksters – and the end of the
road for dropouts who can't make the grade? I decided
to do some research, to try to trace the Bowery's varie-
gated history.

Manhattan's geography destined the ridge running its
length to become a thoroughfare. Long before Europeans
arrived, native peoples traversed the Wickquasgeck
Trail through forests of poplar, pine, oak, and chestnut,
hunting for game, harvesting nuts and berries, or fishing
inlets at the island's edge.[6]

The arrival of the Dutch in 1613 drastically changed
the lives and lands of the native population. The settlers
established Fort Amsterdam at Manhattan's southern
tip, as a base from which to expand their conquest. At
this trading post, the story goes, Peter Minuit of the
Dutch West India Company made his notorious deal in
the 1620s, obtaining Manhattan Island from the Lenape
tribe for sixty guilders' worth of trinkets (approximately
twenty-four dollars in today's currency). The National
Museum of the American Indian now occupies the likely
site of this exchange – an irony that seems to elude both
historians and tourists.

The Dutch had their African slaves widen the
Wickquasgeck Trail to connect the colony at New

Amsterdam with a group of bouweries, or farms, about a
mile north. The Dutch West India Company then freed
some of these slaves, but it was a provisional freedom: the
Africans had to give a portion of their labor and crops to
the colonists. Their settlement also conveniently shielded
the Europeans when Native Americans attacked.[7] The
former slaves thrived, however, establishing a prosperous
community within ten years.[8]

After the British took control of the island, renaming
New Amsterdam "New York" in 1664, they became
alarmed at the former slaves' growing prosperity. In the
early 1700s, they seized the Africans' lands,[9] forcing
them to move beside the Collect, a forty-eight-acre pond.
This was the island's only freshwater source, which the
settlers had polluted – near what would later become
the Five Points slum. (In the early nineteenth century
this pond was filled in, and the prison known as the
Tombs was built on the site.) When the Redcoats were
vanquished in 1783, George Washington and his men
celebrated their departure with a glass of ale at Bull's
Head Tavern on the Bowery.[10]

Although not obvious, reminders of the area's early
African population can still be found. Freeman Alley,
dating back to the 1600s and named for the colony of
freed slaves, runs directly behind the Mission. There used
to be an African burial ground too, where Sara Roosevelt Park now lies. In 1853 the bodies were exhumed and
the cemetery closed,[11] but a secluded garden, M'Finda

Kalunga – meaning "Garden at the Edge of the Other Side of the World" in Kikongo – still honors these original African residents.

If there was ever a melting pot in the United States, it was the Bowery. By the 1800s, poor and working-class Irish, Italians, Chinese, Germans, and Africans interacted on Bowery Lane, as the street was then known. The influx of newcomers and ideas formed fertile ground for the young nation's developing culture, and the Bowery became New York City's first entertainment district.

The four-thousand-seat Bowery Theatre – for a time the largest in the country – opened in the 1840s, and the Windsor Theatre gave audiences some of the country's first performances of Mozart and Wagner. Henry Miner founded Miner's Theater (featuring W. C. Fields, among other famous actors), where the vaudeville hook was devised, a sort of shepherd's crook for removing actors when they fell from audience favor.[12] Tony Pastor, the "Father of Vaudeville," directed the Opera House, which opened on the Bowery in 1865.

The local population also enjoyed Shakespeare plays and contemporary drama; even bootblacks and newsboys could afford balcony seats. A theatrical version of *Uncle Tom's Cabin* premiered on the Bowery a year after the book's 1852 publication.[13]

African Americans took their place on Bowery stages nearly eighty years before Broadway integrated. One of the best known, William Henry Lane (a.k.a. Master Juba), was performing in Five Points establishments by age fifteen. Acclaimed alike by Americans and visiting Europeans – Charles Dickens among them – Lane is believed to have invented tap dancing, by fusing African shuffles with Irish jigs.[14]

Over the years, the Bowery continued to play a role in American history. Abraham Lincoln's anti-slavery speech at Cooper Union helped propel him to the presidency. Even John Brown, who tried to overthrow slavery through armed insurrection, found his way there, albeit posthumously; his body was taken to a Bowery Quaker undertaker after his execution.

Meanwhile, tough Irish-American youth known as Bowery boys and girls – "b'hoys" and "g'hals," in their brogue – were establishing their identity through fashion, slang, alcohol, drugs, crime, and gambling sports like horse racing and bare-knuckle boxing. Words and phrases popularized by the Bowery boys and girls still echo in American vernacular: chum, pal, going on a bender, blowout, kick the bucket, out of sight.[15]

Literature, as well as language, has been marked by the Bowery's grit and grandeur. In "The Old Bowery," Walt Whitman describes the impact its theater district had on his youth.

> It was at the Bowery I first saw Edwin Forrest (the play was John Howard Payne's "Brutus, or the Fall

of Tarquin," and it affected me for weeks, or rather I
might say permanently filter'd into my whole nature),
then in the zenith of his fame and ability. Sometimes
(perhaps a veteran's benefit night) the Bowery would
group together five or six of the first-class actors of those
days – Booth, Forrest, Cooper, Hamblin, and John R.
Scott, for instance. At that time and here George Jones
("Count Joannes") was a young, handsome actor, and
quite a favorite. I remember seeing him in the title role
in "Julius Caesar," and a capital performance it was.[16]

Although from Brooklyn, Whitman used Bowery jargon,
belonging as he did to the lower middle class. When
reviewing his first edition of *Leaves of Grass,* the *New
York Daily News* nicknamed him the b'hoy poet. "So
Long," the title of one of his verses, is an expression that
came from the Bowery. The poem reads:

> I announce a life that shall be copious, vehement, spiri-
> tual, bold;
> I announce an end that shall lightly and joyfully meet its
> translation;
> I announce myriads of youths, beautiful, gigantic,
> sweet-blooded;
> I announce a race of splendid and savage old men.
> O thicker and faster! (So long!)
> O crowding too close upon me;
> I foresee too much – it means more than I thought;
> It appears to me I am dying.[17]

As the nation moved toward civil war, the Bowery started gaining a reputation for vice and violence. Gangs like the Dead Rabbits and Bowery Boys – in which Al Capone was a street tough – clashed over control of Five Points, then occupied mainly by Irish immigrants and free Africans. Named for its location at the intersection of Little Water, Anthony, Cross, Orange, and Mulberry streets, the district was marked by brothels and bars. Elmer Bendiner, author of *The Bowery Man,* wrote:

> The passions of the Bowery in the years before the war mix with the overcharged emotions of abolitionists and Know-Nothings. On July 4, 1857, the Dead Rabbits, mostly Irish, and the Bowery Boys, prideful native Americans [that is, born in America], stage a spectacular holiday display. Beginning at one o'clock in the morning, the bricks fly. Barricades go up. Policemen go down like flies. People are hurled from rooftops. Stores are broken into, and free-lancers who care for neither the Rabbits nor the Boys, nor anything at all save loot, have a field day.[18]

Despite these changes, the Bowery still produced one of America's great songwriters. Born in 1888, Irving Berlin authored more than fifteen hundred songs during his sixty-year career – including familiars like "White Christmas" and "There's no business like show business" – plus scores for Broadway shows and Hollywood films. He had dropped out of school as an eight-year-old to sell newspapers along the Bowery, earning a few extra coins by singing songs he picked up outside its bars. At fourteen he quit selling papers, moved into a lodging house, and became a singing waiter.

By the time Berlin left the street, however, its golden age of music and theater was over. In the 1880s, rich men in white gloves were engaging in excess at glittering establishments on the upper Bowery, while the destitute did likewise at the lower end, in grubby gin mills and gambling halls with names like The Ruins and Milligans' Hell.

The Gilded Age[19] led the country into a new century – gilded, because much of the nation subsisted in poverty while the upper class built showy mansions. Civil War veterans came to New York looking for work, lodging, and entertainment. Historian Theresa Noonan writes, "the Bowery became known for its cheap amusements . . . as music halls, dramatic theaters, and German beer halls shared the street with dive bars, taxi dance halls, pawnbrokers, medicine shows, confidence men, and 'museums' featuring sword swallowers, exotic animals, and scantily-clad women."[20]

Stephen Crane's 1893 novel, *Maggie: A Girl of the Streets,* depicts the region's privation and depravity. Even in Ireland, James Joyce referenced the street in his *Ulysses:* "Ignatius Gallaher we all know and his Chapelizod boss, Harmsworth of the farthing press, and his American cousin of the Bowery gutter sheet."

The hit song of 1891, from Charles Hoyt's Broadway musical, *A Trip to Chinatown,* had six stanzas describing the district's demise. Each chorus repeated, "The Bowery, the Bowery, I'll never go there anymore."

To make matters worse, Noonan writes, "with the opening of the Third Avenue Elevated along the Bowery in 1878, the street was cast into permanent shadow, and pedestrians were showered with hot cinders from the steam trains running above and next to the sidewalks."[21] Those riding the El, as it was known, traveled in comfort, but the racket and soot were harsh for families doubled up in small apartments below and for occupants of Bowery flophouses. In my early years at the Mission, I got to know Tommy Dix, a man in his nineties, who remembered the Bowery's dismal aura before the El was demolished in 1955. "It was a horrible place," he told me with a shudder.

Meanwhile, fleeing persecution or poverty in their homelands, Jews, Lithuanians, Armenians, Poles, Romanians, Scandinavians, and more Irish flocked to the United States. More than twelve million arrived between 1890 and 1910,[22] most landing (and many staying) in New York City. Thousands crammed into the slums of Manhattan's Lower East Side.

On November 7, 1879, a group of men and women gathered in a rented room at 14 Bowery. Though few in number, they were strong in purpose as they prayed for souls trapped in poverty and sin.[23] This meeting, led by Reverend Albert Ruliffson, launched the Bowery Mission.

Albert Gleason Ruliffson was born on his grandfather's farm, south of Albany, in 1833. After university, he spent some years as principal of rural New York schools, until his faith spurred him to enter the ministry and he enrolled in Union Theological Seminary (my alma mater as well). After ordination, Albert married Ellen Dorchester, a teacher eight years his senior, and in 1862 he enlisted in the Union Army as a chaplain. After the Civil War, a Presbyterian agency in Minnesota tasked him with evangelizing settlements there – strengthening weak churches, building new ones, and raising up ministers. The couple next moved to Chicago, then back to New York in the early 1870s.

Paving the way for the social gospel movement, the Ruliffsons, together with other Protestant progressives, challenged the social structures that perpetuated gambling, prostitution, alcoholism, and drug abuse. Albert founded the Bethany Institute, a women's missionary training center. Ellen was active in prohibition. She and others would enter saloons to disrupt decadence, preach against liquor, and proclaim new life through repentance.

Albert and Ellen Ruliffson knew some of the most influential Christians of their day. As the *New York Times*[24] reported, Rev. Ruliffson offered the prayer at one of Dwight L. Moody's revival meetings. Yet it was not from eminent evangelists that the Ruliffsons sought advice; it was ex-convict Jeremiah McAuley who inspired them to action. Founder of the gospel rescue mission movement, McAuley had long hoped an outpost would open on the Bowery. The Ruliffsons fulfilled his dream.

"God uses the foolish things of this world to confound the wise,"[25] could apply to the story of Jeremiah McAuley. He was born in Ireland in 1839. By the time he turned twenty, he had immigrated to the United States, been convicted of highway robbery, and found himself sentenced to ten years in Sing Sing. He was converted in prison, on hearing the testimony of a former boxer, Orville "the Awful" Gardener. On his release, McAuley vowed to minister to the "least of these."[26] He opened his first rescue mission, Helping Hand for Men, in 1872. (It was later renamed McAuley Water Street Mission, then New York City Rescue Mission. In 2017, it was incorporated into the Bowery Mission.) Today there are hundreds of similar rescue missions worldwide.

Owen Kildare, the so-called "Kipling of the Bowery," describes the street around the time the Ruliffsons began their work:

In that one block, between Chatham Square to Bayard Street, were eight concert halls; five gambling houses; four fake museums – blinds for lottery schemes or indecent exhibitions; seven saloons, not one of them conducted legitimately; nine 'hotels' of the rankest sort; five lodging houses, ranging in price from twenty-five to seven cents; while in the adjoining block, in Bayard Street, every house – without exception – was a den of ill-repute. In addition it must be mentioned that the Whyo gang, the Cherry Hill gang, and the Five Points gang had their headquarters there, and sometimes worked in concert to the discomfort of peaceful citizens, and, again, fought their battles in pitched array to the bodily injury of inoffensive non-participants.[27]

By this time, many Christians thought Manhattan's Lower East Side was beyond hope, but Albert Ruliffson declared, "If I could be the means, under God, of establishing a mission on the Bowery, that is all I would ask on earth." And indeed, the flame that flickered to life here, in November 1879, continues to burn brightly fourteen decades later.

The Ruliffsons led the Bowery Mission until they left New York City in 1895, due to Albert's ill health. He died two years later, but Ellen continued to support the Bowery Mission, dividing her time between Utica and Manhattan for the next eighteen years. She died in 1915 at age ninety, among the last from that first generation of Mission workers.

Before moving to its current location at Number 227 Bowery, the Mission occupied several sites. That first year its foundation was laid, at Number 14: proclamation of repentance and God's forgiving love. In its second year, the Mission expanded to a second building, Number 36, where meals were provided at nominal cost. (There were plenty of cheap diners on the street, but they lured their customers with alcohol, gambling, and prostitution.)

In 1887, the functions of Numbers 14 and 36 were consolidated at Number 105. This five-story brick building, known as the Bastille of the Bowery, had been owned and run by bareknuckle champ Owney Geoghegan.[28] His Gas House Gang, which eventually merged with the Five Points Gang, operated brothels and was infamous for committing forty robberies in one night.

At the Bastille, Geoghegan sold raw whiskey, distilled on site, for ten cents a shot. Rowdy customers abetted nightly boxing matches, some featuring female boxers. If no one stepped into the ring, barrel-chested bartenders provided the entertainment. The saloon was so chaotic, Geoghegan "had no less than 102 indictments against him and his license was constantly revoked."[29] It closed after his death in 1885. Two years later the Bowery Mission moved in, redeeming Number 105 from its sordid reputation. But the following year, in March 1898, disaster struck.

The building's first floor contained the hall where Mission services were conducted. The upper four levels held up to forty beds each, separated by flimsy partitions. More than one hundred and fifty men were sleeping there when John Sullivan, a boarder on the fourth story, woke at 1:30 a.m. to the smell of smoke. He cried out, and both he and the night clerk dashed to the top floor, waking sleepers as they ran – hoping to hurry back down to find and extinguish the fire. But flames spread quickly between the partitions, occupants stampeded, and some were trampled or burned in the rush to get out. Most had undressed before bed in the stuffy quarters, and naked men now burst into nearby restaurants and lodging houses, hiding behind counters until clothes or blankets were thrown to them.

According to the *New York Times,* the fire began when a boarder on the third floor lit a match for his pipe and thoughtlessly dropped it on a pile of papers. "Groups that reached the windows beat out the glass with their hands and arms, and then there were fighting and crushing, shrieking and howling, among the terrified men to get to the fire escape."[30]

At 1:40 a.m. a patrol officer saw flames shooting from a third floor window and dispatched the fire brigade. Hook and Ladder Companies 6 and 9, as well as Engines 9, 55, and 17 responded to the first alarm. Their arrival was followed by a second and third alarm, which brought nine additional engines. The firemen rescued many lodgers and fought for hours to bring the blaze under control.

When the fire was finally extinguished, the search for bodies began. Eleven were found, but only three were identified: John Foran, a twenty-eight-year-old machinist from Staten Island; William McDermott, a twenty-six-year-old painter from Brooklyn; and William Sodan, a thirty-eight-year-old New Jersey farmer. That eight remain unknown underscores the fact that, for many, being homeless means being nameless.

The fire pressured officials to revise the building code. "While it is generally acknowledged that the law was complied with in this instance and the lodging house was one of the best of its kind, the catastrophe, it is said, has shown that the laws upon the statute books are entirely inadequate," stated the *New York Times*.[31]

The Mission's parent organization, the Christian Herald, occupied three buildings along the Bowery by this time. After the fire, Mission services consolidated into one of these, 55 Bowery, operating from there for the following years. In 1905, however, construction of the Manhattan Bridge meant that many buildings were razed, including Number 55.[32] The Mission took temporary residence at 37 Bowery, while renovating Number 227 – its current location – to which it moved on November 7, 1909. (In 1980 the Mission acquired the adjacent building, Number 229, and merged it with 227. In the nineteenth century, 229 had been occupied by photographer Charles Eisenmann, hired by P. T. Barnum to make postcards of sideshow performers like Jojo the Dog-faced Boy or Siamese twins Chang and Eng.)

During the latter half of the twentieth century – thanks to the Bowery's cheap real estate values, and despite its skid-row reputation – numerous writers and musicians moved into the area, making it once more an artists' enclave. Roy Lichtenstein, Robert Frank, William Burroughs, Amiri Baraka, Maya Lin, Debbie Harry, and Jean-Michel Basquiat were among them.[33] Mark Rothko lived right across from the Mission, at 222 Bowery; William Seward Burroughs – beat author of *Junkie* and *Naked Lunch* – occupied that building from 1966 until his death in 1997.[34]

Allen Ginsberg's epic poem "Howl," written in 1956, pays homage to Bowery drifters:

> . . . their heads shall be crowned with laurel in oblivion,
> who ate the lamb stew of the imagination or digested
>   the crab at the muddy bottom of the rivers of Bowery,
> who wept at the romance of the streets with their
>   pushcarts full of onions and bad music,
> who sat in boxes breathing in the darkness under
>   the bridge, and rose up to build harpsichords in
>   their lofts . . .

Beat Generation authors romanticized Bowery bums, whose lifestyle resonated with their own culture. Jack Kerouac, self-proclaimed king of the beats, titled one collection of poetry *Bowery Blues,* and in 1960 he penned an article, "The Vanishing American Hobo," that included interviews with men at the Bowery Mission. Kerouac wrote:

> The Bowery is the haven for hobos who came to the big city to make the big time by getting pushcarts and collecting cardboard. – Lots of Bowery bums are Scandinavian, lots of them bleed easily because they drink too much. – When winter comes bums drink a drink called smoke, it consists of wood alcohol and a drop of iodine and a scab of lemon, this they gulp down and wham! they hibernate all winter so as not to catch cold, because they don't live anywhere, and it gets very cold outside in the city in winter. – Sometimes hobos sleep arm-in-arm to keep warm, right on the sidewalk. Bowery Mission veterans say that the beer-drinking bums are the most belligerent of the lot.[35]

In the 1970s, disenchanted with Greenwich Village folk rock and the disco-decade, New York teenagers unleashed the punk rock movement. CBGB, the iconic club that opened at 315 Bowery in 1973, embodied the new scene. This was the launch pad for Blondie, The Ramones, Talking Heads, Patti Smith, and similar acts. Like the Bowery Boys before them, punk youth infused popular culture with their music, fashion, and slang.

Meanwhile, the Bowery Mission was struggling. Addiction to heroin and other opioids had continued to rise. In the 1960s, the Mission allowed the Clinic of Narcotic Drug Control to operate daily on site, and introduced Narcotics Anonymous alongside Alcoholics Anonymous.

The sixties had begun with a tragedy for the Mission. Early in the morning of January 9, 1960, approximately one hundred homeless men were in the dormitory below the chapel when one of them pulled a seven-inch blade and threatened the others, preventing anyone from leaving. The *New York Times* reported, "The derelicts were cowering in a semi-circle around the thug, some on newspapers they were using as sleeping mats, others crouched on the floor."

Sergeant Edward Johnson and three patrolmen had just broken up a fight at the Salvation Army next door when the Mission's resident manager called for help. Johnson came immediately but was attacked as he entered the dorm.

"Drop it. Drop it or I'll shoot," the sergeant ordered, pointing at the knife with his pistol.

"No. No. I won't. You'll have to come and get it," the assailant yelled. Then, lunging at the sergeant, he screamed, "I'm coming for you."

The attacker stabbed Johnson in the chest. As the sergeant fell, he "fired six evenly spaced, carefully aimed shots. Another policeman at his shoulder fired three more." Four of the sergeant's bullets hit the assailant. Minutes later both were dead.[36]

The nature of homelessness altered significantly around this time. When the Bowery Mission first opened, the hobo stereotype was a white middle-aged male alcoholic. In the latter half of the twentieth century, however, people of Irish, Italian, and Scandinavian descent were moving out of the inner city, replaced by African Americans, Hispanics, and non-European immigrants. In 1970 whites still comprised about 50 percent of the men using New York City shelters, while 36 percent were African American. Today approximately 8 percent are white, 58 percent African American, and 31 percent Hispanic. Less than 1 percent are Asian, while 3 percent are of unknown ethnicity.[37] This is comparable to what we currently see at the Mission.

In 1976, 31 percent of New York City shelter clients had a history of hospitalization in state mental institutions, and another 22 percent said they had been diagnosed as mentally disabled.[38] Those figures swelled a few years later, as mental health facilities downsized (or closed) when the Reagan administration cut their funding. Many patients wound up on the street, with little or no support. In response to this growing crisis, in the 1980s the Mission began to develop a clinical/pastoral approach to support the mentally ill.

Around the same time, the number of homeless women increased, and the "bag lady" became a familiar sight in American cities. While service providers across the country wrestled with how to respond to the demographic changes, a shift in sentiment undermined their support. The public increasingly blamed the poor for their problems, labeling them as lazy or as abusers of social services, as exemplified in prevalent "welfare queen" myths.

During these years, the Mission gradually blended into the grimy cityscape. The chapel's stained glass windows were almost concealed by a fire escape, erected in the 1950s or '60s, and the continuous traffic of destitute men took its toll. They kept coming – or returning – knowing they'd be offered free food, shaves, and showers. If a man came back a second night, he became eligible for a bed and locker upstairs; if he continued to show that he was serious, he was sent to the Mission's Midtown rooming house, which accommodated thirty men. Here, for five dollars per week, he could stay for a month, during which he had to find work and move on. This basic program continued until the early 1990s, when the emphasis shifted. Where the Mission had sheltered 276 men per night in February 1964, in 1990 it sheltered only fifteen, while providing a wider range of services.[39]

CHRISTIAN
AND SIGNS

COPYRI

ME 19.

NEW YORK.

. DE WITT TALMAGE, D. D., Editor.
es :— Bible House, New York City.

ℌERALD

UR TIMES

s KLOPSCH.

NUMBER

H 11, 1896

NUMBER

3 **Magazine with a Mission**

Just as a converted highway robber inspired the Bowery Mission's start, so it was through a drunken sailor that its fiscal stability was eventually secured.

In 1885 John Parkinson, a British seaman, headed for the Bowery, elated to be on land after weeks on the ocean. A few hours later, his walk was wobbling:

> One of the earliest converts of the Mission was a drunken sailor, who staggered into the little room thinking it was a music hall. His ship was then lying in the docks, and he, following the usual routine of sailors ashore, had been visiting the saloons and dives of the Bowery. He was so helplessly intoxicated that he was kept in the Mission all night, and as a result was clearly and happily converted to Christ.

Returning to sea, Parkinson preached the gospel wherever he went. While his ship was docked at Smyrna (now Izmir, Turkey), he joined an English-speaking mission there called the Seamen's Institute. He eventually became its leader.

Ten years after Parkinson's conversion, Louis Klopsch, publisher and proprietor of the *Christian Herald* – one of America's most influential religious magazines – was touring the Mediterranean with his friend Thomas De Witt Talmage, coeditor of the magazine and renowned American preacher, and their wives. In the course of their travels, the couples arrived at Smyrna, where Parkinson invited them to address the sailors at the Seamen's Institute. Parkinson then told Klopsch and Talmage about his experience on the Bowery. Klopsch, a New Yorker, had never heard of the Bowery Mission, but Parkinson's testimony so intrigued him that he returned home determined to look it up. When he did so, he discovered that the Mission had fallen on hard times.

At the Ruliffsons' retirement earlier in 1895, they had left a superintendent in charge, but he had unexpectedly died some months later. So, when Klopsch came to see the place Parkinson had described, he found that with its organizational challenges, lack of leadership, and the ongoing effects of the 1893 financial panic, the Mission was in danger of closing its doors forever.

Grasping the situation, Klopsch decided to purchase the Mission. He became its president, organized its first board of directors, and filed its articles of incorporation. From this time on, the Bowery Mission's ministry proceeded under the Christian Herald organization.

Klopsch's magazine, the *Christian Herald and Signs of Our Times,* had been established in England in 1878 by Joseph Spurgeon (cousin of evangelist Charles Spurgeon) and Michael Baxter, an Anglican priest. Magazine contributors included George Müller, who cared for thousands of orphans in England, and American ministers such as Talmage and W. E. Blackstone. The *Herald* soon started publishing an American edition, which before long had a circulation of thirty thousand.

In 1889 Klopsch traveled to England to negotiate with Michael Baxter, took the editorial reins of the magazine's American branch, and subsequently purchased it. Under his direction, the *Herald*'s circulation eventually increased to four hundred thousand, making it the world's most widely read religious publication.

Louis Klopsch was born in 1852 near Berlin. He lost his mother to illness when he was barely a year old. His father, Osmar Klopsch, fled Germany to avoid imprisonment for revolutionary activity, settling in New York with his young son.

Louis Klopsch studied journalism at Columbia University. He then honed his publishing and business skills through the development of *Good Morning,* a devotional journal, and *Daily Hotel Reporter,* a trade magazine. He owned *Pictorial Associated Press* as well, where he pioneered photojournalism.

The nation's conscience was stirring in the late nineteenth century, as Christians wrestled with how to apply gospel teachings to social issues. Some plunged into the temperance movement in efforts to free people

ensnared by alcohol, urging legislation to limit (or
eliminate) its availability. Jane Addams and other
reformers were starting settlement houses to alleviate the
plight of immigrants living in overcrowded tenements
and working in sweatshops. Addams's aspiration – to
bring reading, art, music, drama, nutrition, and physical
education to families in poverty – spread across the
country. The Catholic Worker hospitality houses that
Dorothy Day founded in New York during the Great
Depression continued the concepts Addams had begun
at Chicago's Hull House.

Already in 1879 – the year after the publication's
founding and coincidentally the year the Bowery
Mission began – the *Herald* had lent support to clergy
protesting conditions in Lower East Side tenements.
Jeremiah McAuley took legal action to shut down unsafe
housing, and other rescue mission workers joined the
effort, going into slums to clean squalid rooms, bring
food and fuel, and help evicted or ill-housed families find
decent apartments. Meanwhile, Rev. Talmage preached a
series of sermons deploring the greed of New York land-
lords. This was the first political action with which the
Herald's editors aligned the magazine, and their efforts
eventually bore fruit. In 1901 the New York State Tenement House Act was passed, one of the first laws to
regulate building code. From then on, new apartment
blocks were required to have fire escapes, indoor toilets,
and proper ventilation, including a window per room.

Under Klopsch and Talmage's leadership, the *Herald* continued as an instrument of the social gospel movement. With an emphasis on putting faith into action, it promoted causes ranging from labor to women's suffrage. It raised funds to run various ministries and printed articles deploring corporations' "right" to acquire labor at the cheapest possible price. Its editorials backed legislation to outlaw the seven-day workweek, protect children in industry, compensate injured workers, and support struggling farmers. During the drought of 1895, the magazine organized the Western Farmers' Relief Fund for homesteaders in Colorado, the Dakotas, Kansas, and Nebraska.

The *Herald*'s circulation kept increasing, thanks to its photojournalism and its articles by Talmage and Spurgeon. Theologically conservative but socially progressive, Spurgeon struck a nerve with Christians on both sides of the Atlantic. Many of his *Herald* articles reflected his anti-imperialist views and opposition to war.

The *Herald*'s first international relief effort began in 1892, when Klopsch and Talmage brought the Russian famine into American homes through graphic photos. The editors included articles by Leo Tolstoy, a respected Russian novelist. Through the following years, most of the *Herald*'s relief work was overseas – in China, India, Japan, Sweden, Finland, and elsewhere. Klopsch usually channeled readers' aid through the State Department, but he often went to affected regions himself to supervise distribution. Returning to New York, he would write descriptive articles petitioning readers' continued support. From 1892 to 1910, the *Herald*'s readers provided the equivalent of over eighty million dollars in today's currency for relief and mission work.

The *Herald*'s first domestic ministry began during the harsh winter of 1894, when the magazine established a food fund for New York City's poor and immigrant communities. There was such an outpouring of donations, Klopsch used the surplus to organize summer outings for Lower East Side children at Mont Lawn Fresh Air Home in Nyack, New York – the birth of the fresh air movement.

The *Herald* eventually purchased the estate, later renamed Mont Lawn Camp. Jacob Riis – whose 1890 classic, *How the Other Half Lives,* had alerted the nation to tenement conditions – dedicated the camp's chapel in 1905. (In the 1960s, the camp relocated to two hundred acres in the Poconos. Today, apart from serving more than a thousand children each summer, the property doubles as an off-season retreat center. Bowery Mission staff also operate City Camp, to provide year-round academic mentorship.)

Louis Klopsch remained active until his death in 1910. Talmage died in 1902, after passing his task to George Sandison, a longtime contributor. Sandison carried on the magazine's tradition of challenging Christians, declaring in a 1916 editorial that the church had "too often misunderstood and neglected and alienated the laborers." Sandison's editorship, from 1902 to 1920, included World War I and its aftermath, when the *Herald* backed disarmament and established the Relief Fund for Widows and Orphans.

After Sandison, Charles Sheldon was editor-in-chief from 1920 to 1925, and he remained a contributing editor until his death in 1946. He had already been connected with the magazine for some years and "commended the *Herald* for its firm stand at a time when most Eastern dailies and a number of religious journals were 'preaching war.'" In 1915, the *Herald* printed an open letter from Sheldon to President Wilson, who had used the Bible to defend militarism. Sheldon's letter argued that Christ would surely promote "justice and brother-hood" rather than military might. The *Herald* had also published one of his poems:

> My brother, of whatever tongue or race
> Whatever be the color of thy skin
> Tho' either white or black or brown thy face
> Thou art in God's great family – my kin.

A Kansas pastor, Sheldon is best known as the author of *In His Steps,* or *What Would Jesus Do?,* which has sold more than fifty million copies since its 1896 publication. Influenced by Walter Rauschenbusch, architect of the social gospel, Sheldon emphasized that Christians' lives must align with their beliefs. He remained a lifelong pacifist, vegetarian, and activist for racial and gender equality.

From Spurgeon and Klopsch to Sandison and Sheldon, the *Herald*'s early leaders challenged complacent American Christianity. Sheldon was succeeded by Daniel Poling. The two men had cooperated as early as 1914 (when both advocated for prohibition), and they wrote forewords for each other's books into the 1940s. Yet the magazine took a decidedly different course after Poling took the reins. He was editor for nearly forty years, from 1927 to 1966.

As well as authoring twenty-two books, Poling was active in politics, starting in 1912 when he was Prohibition Party candidate for Ohio Governor (he lost). In 1951, he unsuccessfully ran for mayor of Philadelphia on the Republican ticket, after which President Truman tasked him with investigating administration tax scandals. He then served on the President's Civilian Advisory Commission on universal military training.

A senior pastor at Marble Collegiate from 1920 to 1930, Poling remained active there after being succeeded by Norman Vincent Peale, renowned for his *Power of Positive Thinking*. Where the social gospel led to liberation theology, "positive thinking" is considered a precursor of the prosperity gospel. Franklin D. Roosevelt called Poling "America's spiritual ambassador for good will," and on Poling's eightieth birthday a *Time* article called him a "gentle fundamentalist."

Gentle as it may have seemed, Poling's fundamentalism was a stark departure from the magazine's initial direction. A military chaplain during both World Wars, he made six overseas missions during World War II and visited all active theaters of operation. He shifted the *Herald*'s view to endorse United States' military interventions, the draft, and development of the atomic bomb.

In 1939 Poling purchased and restructured the *Herald,* which was then in financial straits. Under his leadership, the organization focused on the magazine – growing its circulation to an unprecedented four hundred and fifty thousand – but quit most of its international relief work. It did, however, continue to support Mont Lawn Camp and the Bowery Mission. By the 1960s, Mont Lawn was flourishing. The Mission, on the other hand, seemed little more than a Christian flophouse.

Like Klopsch, Poling was a strong leader. After his death in 1968, later editors lacked the charisma to sustain the magazine's influence. Its circulation dwindled, and the Bowery Mission fought to stay afloat.

Two presidents who have led the organization in the twenty-first century, Edward Morgan and David Jones, have turned this situation around. Morgan, son of a Princeton Presbyterian minister, was a nominal Christian until he felt a personal call to serve Christ in 1986. He joined the Christian Herald organization's board of directors, and in 1994 he became its president, entering this ministry after a career at General Electric – and accepting a 55 percent pay cut in doing so. He led for twenty years.

The magazine was foundering when Morgan took the helm, and the Bowery Mission had a five hundred thousand dollar deficit and a rapidly dwindling endowment. Realizing that more people were interested in donating to the Bowery Mission than in subscribing to (or reading) the *Herald,* Morgan proposed dissolving the magazine in favor of developing the Mission's programs. Ever since his forward-thinking act, the Christian Herald name has been used almost exclusively for legal documents.

Under Morgan's leadership, the organization doubled its income in a decade; during his last three years as president, he "led a successful campaign that raised more than ten million dollars, expanded the Bowery Mission into three new neighborhoods, and doubled its capacity for transforming the lives of New York's most vulnerable children and homeless adults." The five recovery programs he developed included Manhattan's only faith-based residential programs for women.

A major boon was the 1996 acquisition of a sixty-bed shelter in Alphabet City, lower Manhattan. When Morgan signed the contract, however, it stated that the place had to be operated under New York City's Department of Homeless Services for twenty years. In 2016, it became Bowery Mission property. Now at last the gospel is freely shared at this top-rated facility, free from secular guidelines. Many faith-based nonprofits have gone the secular route in recent years for the sake of funding, but the Bowery Mission's board of directors has kept the organization firmly on its Christian foundation.

In 2015 Morgan passed the presidency to David Jones. Both men have addressed root causes of homelessness, and both have ensured that Bowery Mission guests can join the residential program for up to a year or more, receiving one-on-one counseling and accessing support groups; wellness classes; and workshops in monetary management, vocational training, and independent living.

Although new to homeless ministry, Jones brought passion for the work and experience of the corporate world. He grew up in Florida, unchurched and poor. When he asked, as a teenager, "How can I get rich?" his high school guidance counselor suggested finance – and Jones took the advice. He graduated from Florida State University and later earned his MBA at Columbia University. He then worked with an international accounting firm, KPMG, for twenty-six years, eventually becoming a partner. But while he had achieved his ambition, life seemed empty. Trying to fill the void, Jones drank to excess, and was eventually caught driving while intoxicated.

Jones came to faith in Christ at Trinity Baptist Church in New York City. After the DWI charge, he fulfilled his community service obligation at the Bowery Mission's Alphabet City campus – his first encounter with the organization he would eventually lead. Jones next pursued theology, first at Alliance Theological Seminary and then at Princeton, after which he served a nondenominational church in New Jersey for six years. After retiring from KPMG, he became interim president of Goodwill Rescue Mission until assuming presidency of the Bowery Mission on Morgan's retirement.

Understanding acquisitions and mergers, organizational development, and the importance of fiscal viability – and striving to fulfill the organization's mission statement to be the "most effective provider of compassionate care and life transformation services for hurting people in New York City" – Jones redesigned programs to match the new sites Morgan had acquired.

During his first two years in charge, Jones adopted two struggling missions: Goodwill Rescue Mission in Newark, New Jersey, and New York City Rescue Mission, which Jeremiah McAuley had founded in 1872 as the first-ever rescue mission. Thus, the Bowery Mission now consists of nine facilities in the tri-state area, besides its midtown headquarters.

Having blazed the trail for modern journalism and charitable fundraising as an influential religious magazine, the *Christian Herald* lives on in the work of the Bowery Mission.

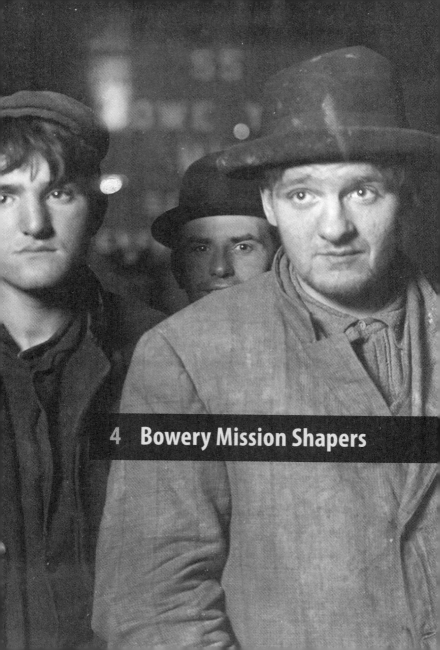

4 Bowery Mission Shapers

Throughout the Bowery Mission's one hundred and forty years, colorful characters of every stripe – evangelists and eccentrics, politicians and athletes – have lent their support, each leaving an imprint. But it was the on-the-ground daily leadership of the Mission's superintendents that most shaped its character. Although backed by Christian Herald leaders, their task was far plainer and more practical.

There have been eleven superintendents in all (see appendix timeline). The first, Josiah Childs, held the post for less than a year; he died of influenza just months after his appointment in 1895. John Greener Hallimond, appointed in 1899, served twenty-five years, the longest of any superintendent. It was he who welcomed John Goode to the Bowery Mission.

Born in 1852 in northern England, Hallimond became an evangelist at age seventeen and worked at the West London Mission under Hugh Price Hughes, a noncon-formist Methodist who challenged the rich to repent. Hallimond later qualified as Doctor of Divinity in

the city of Durham, where he met and married Annie
Foggitt. They had two children.

Moving to the United States in the 1890s, Hallimond, a
"big, smiling Englishman, broad-shouldered and strong-
limbed,"[1] joined the Salvation Army and worked under
Commander Ballington Booth (son of Salvation Army
founders, William and Catherine). In 1895, at Booth's
request, Hallimond established Volunteers of America
social work programs in churches across the country.
Taking on the Bowery Mission was a natural next step.

Of the down-and-outs he met on the Bowery, Hallimond wrote:

> In the early days we dealt with a horde of what some
> called "old bums." Most of them carried tomato cans
> under their coats, which they used in getting the dregs of
> beer kegs that were piled outside the ubiquitous saloon.
> All in all, they were a hard crowd, and so poor that we
> fed a thousand nightly in our bread lines.[2]

Hallimond introduced this free service in 1904. It
continued each winter, from Thanksgiving until April 1,
right through the Great Depression. Around midnight,
hungry men would start queuing on the Bowery or in
Freeman Alley. Some might doze, hunkered on the sidewalk or slumped against a wall, until the chapel opened
at one o'clock and they all surged in.[3] Occasionally there
was exhortation and singing, but at this night hour most

people were interested only in the rolls and hot coffee. The first year, one hundred and twenty-nine thousand breakfasts were given out. By 1913 the number had risen to two hundred thousand, with a daily average of over fifteen hundred.[4]

Superintendent Hallimond led nightly chapel services and devoted an evening per week to citizenship training. He knew, however, that his listeners' fragile faith would be severely tested. "A Bowery congregation is such a crowd of transients," he wrote, pondering how to help. "Men pass on so quickly, and we never see them again. What we needed was something that would bind them together in some firm and loving bond, from the moment they declared themselves as Christians."[5]

In 1907, Hallimond forged a plan. At the end of service one evening, he asked "if there was any man present who felt the need of a brother; if so, and he would come forward, I would shake his hand and pledge myself to become a brother to him."[6] Twenty men responded. They decided to meet each evening, an hour before chapel. Thus the Brotherhood of the Bowery was formed.

Participants shared their histories, encouraged each other, and prayed together. Regardless of what a man had done, he was considered a brother. Each was given a membership card and assured that the others would pray for him. Becoming a card-carrying member was not hard: the only requirement was to accept the card at the evening service and return the next night. Yet for many, this was a decisive first step.

Over time, seasoned brothers helped new members back onto their feet, while the novices' enthusiasm kept the movement fresh. Hallimond tried to maintain contact with them all, noting any change of address; his records show that many stayed on the straight path.[7] Toward the end of his life, he wrote, "We avoid all emotional methods and simply ask a man to sign, as a member of our brotherhood. That organization now has a membership of 42,000."[8]

Hallimond realized that there was need for "a home in which could be gathered the converts."[9] So when a wealthy widower told him, "Hallimond, this is an awful thing that has come to me. I must get busy, I must get some new work, I must do something to help other suffering men,"[10] Hallimond proposed a plan. The widower agreed, and Memorial House was opened on East Broadway. In 1909 it moved to 227 Bowery, becoming the Winner's Club – dubbed "a home for self-supporting men" in religious periodicals – a prototype for the Mission's residential programs ever since. In 1905, Bethesda Home opened briefly in Brooklyn to provide shelter and discipleship training for women as well.[11]

The Mission's Labor Bureau was also established around this time, operating five days a week and providing free transportation as far as fifty miles. Within

ten years, more than twenty-five thousand men found
work through the Bureau.

Another outgrowth of Hallimond's Brotherhood
was the Prayer League, announced in a 1914 issue of the
Christian Herald:

> Will you join the Christian Herald Prayer League?
> The correspondence of our Answered Prayer Column
> has demonstrated that prayer holds a very large place
> in the lives of the members of the Christian Herald
> Family. We shall include hereafter in this department
> not only acknowledgments of answered prayer, but also
> requests for prayer. These requests will also be sent to
> the Bowery Mission, where they will be made special
> subjects of supplication at the meetings of the Mission
> brotherhood.[12]

The League maintained an office and met regularly to
pray. They received hundreds of letters weekly from
across the country, such as:

> I wish to tell you your prayers for my little crippled boy
> have been answered. He is now walking, thank God. We
> know God has all power both in heaven and on earth,
> and can and will answer the prayers of His children.
>
> > Mrs. Cornelius Meek,
> > Whitehouse, Kentucky

> I wish to acknowledge a definite answer to prayer. Some
> dishonest men were trying to cheat me out of $300. I
> asked the League to pray that they might not succeed

and, thanks to His holy name, I just got notice that they
had paid in to the bank. I also asked that my wife might
be healed of a disease from which she was suffering
untold agony, and I believe that prayer will be answered
soon, as He has answered hundreds of my prayers.

Louis De Lancett,
Waycross, Georgia[13]

During his quarter century as superintendent, John
Hallimond wrote two books, *The Miracle of Answered
Prayer* and *Greatheart of the Bowery*. After his only
son, William, was killed in Belgium during World War
I, Hallimond had still greater compassion for young
veterans, of whom there were many on the Bowery.
George Sandison, *Christian Herald* editor, said of him:

> They felt his presence as that of a superior who gave
> commands in authoritative fashion, and saw that they
> were carried out. Yet they all knew him for a big, kind-
> hearted leader who would not overlook any waif of the
> street, no matter how dirty and physically repellent
> the man or lad might be. Big John was the friend, the
> adviser, the benefactor of all.[14]

When United States President William Howard Taft
agreed to attend the chapel's dedication in December
1909, hundreds gathered to see and hear him. The
event was scheduled for 9:30 p.m., but minutes – then
hours – ticked by. "The faces were pinched with want,

and some were hardened, too," a reporter noted. "The tattered clothes of the men and boys were rain-soaked."[15]

Superintendent Hallimond and others kept thinking up topics to fill the time until, around eleven o'clock, the President's automobile finally pulled into Freeman Alley. With Klopsch at his side, Taft entered through the chapel's back door and sauntered up the aisle to the preacher's chair on stage.

"My friends, I am just as much surprised at being here as you are to see me," the president told both derelicts and dignitaries. "I had a note from Dr. Klopsch asking me to see the mission, which he had established in the Bowery, after the meeting at Carnegie Hall." In a rousing speech, he then informed the Bowery throng that they were not forgotten.

As the occasion drew to a close, Hallimond asked, "Boys, do you thank the president for coming down to the Bowery tonight?" Six hundred voices chorused, "We do!"[16]

The president wasn't the first or the last unlikely character to address the homeless from the Bowery altar. The illustrious "hobo doctor" Ben Reitman had delivered his anarchist message from the same spot in 1907.[17] Philanthropist Frederick Townsend Martin arrived one evening in 1911, in fur coat and silk hat, to "shake your rough hands as brothers."[18] 'Abdu'l-Bahá, leader of the Baha'i religion, also came that year. New York governor

Plough Quarterly

FREE TRIAL ISSUE

Thank you for your purchase. If you liked this book, you'll want to try our magazine as well. Plough Quarterly brings together a diverse community of readers serious about putting their faith into action. And since you bought one of our books, we'd like to offer one issue free.

Give it a try! Just drop this completed card in the mail, and we'll send you a free trial issue. No cost, no obligation. If you like it, you'll get four more issues for just $18. If you decide not to subscribe, simply write "cancel" on the invoice, return it, and owe nothing. Either way, the trial issue is yours to keep.

Name

Address

City   State   Zip

NO POSTAGE
NECESSARY
IF MAILED
IN THE
UNITED STATES

BUSINESS REPLY MAIL

FIRST-CLASS MAIL   PERMIT NO. 332   CONGERS, NY

POSTAGE WILL BE PAID BY ADDRESSEE

PLOUGH QUARTERLY
PO BOX 345
CONGERS NY 10920-9895

Alfred Smith attended the Mission's fortieth anniversary in 1919, and Franklin D. Roosevelt – then vice presidential nominee – campaigned there the following year.[19] In 1928, blind musician Edwin Grasse played his violin for nearly four hundred listeners after Helen Keller, the first deaf and blind recipient of a bachelor's degree, shared her story.[20]

More than sensational one-time visits from celebrities, however, unnumbered individuals and congregations have impacted the Mission through the chapel services they have faithfully helped to lead three times a day since the outset. Superintendents and staff could not have fulfilled their roles without this participation, most of it unpaid. The first generation of partners, from 1870 to 1915, included a rich lady, an immigrant musician, and a blind poet.

Sarah J. Bird, a former socialite, was a central figure at the Mission for thirty-three years. Won over by reformer Henry Ward Beecher, she became a leader in the abolition, suffrage, and temperance movements. Mother Bird, as she came to be affectionately known, was the only woman to sign the Bowery Mission articles of incorporation. As a founding board member, she knew the Ruliffsons, Klopsch, Talmage, and Hallimond, and she ministered at every Bowery Mission site, from Number 14 to Number 227.

She and her merchant husband, Thomas Bird, had
lived in luxury in Upper Montclair, New Jersey. In 1881,
both began volunteering at the Bowery Mission. When
Thomas died ten years later, she left their wealthy home
to rent a room in the Lower East Side, dropping her
social functions – though not her stately air – to work for
the poor. In *My Old Bailiwick,* Owen Kildare wrote of
Mrs. Bird:

> And there, like in a garden of weeds, among drunkards,
> petty thieves, tramps, and other outcasts, this refined,
> cultured, devoted lady struggled on to reawaken dead-
> ened and shriveled manhood with the messages of
> eternal love. [21]

At the time, the Bowery Mission was one of the few
places to allow women in the pulpit. Without training or
backing from any organization, Mother Bird led services
there from 1881 until 1914, staying each time to give out
lunch or coffee afterward.

Mother Bird also established a kindergarten on the
Bowery, made sure older children went to school, distrib-
uted clothes and medicine, and visited female inmates
at the Tombs. Every Thanksgiving and Christmas, she
made certain the Mission sent food baskets to families
in need. And inside their tenements, she taught mothers
how to sew, prepare healthy meals at low cost, and keep
apartments clean and aired.[22]

John Hallimond described her, "Surrounded by a small group of her devoted coadjutors, Mrs. Bird could be found kneeling on the floor of some cheap lodging house, or in some vicious dive like Suicide Hall, praying for the abandoned men or women, whose salvation she was seeking."[23]

"At the time of Mrs. Bird's death in 1914," historian Norris Magnuson reports, "the Mission noted that of the 24,000 men its labor bureau had placed across the years, everyone who had written back referred greatly to her."[24] After her death, her leadership and motherly constancy were sincerely missed.

In her will, Mother Bird bequeathed three hundred acres in Westchester County to the Mission. Known as Mother Bird Memorial Farm, this Yorktown Heights property included two large farmhouses totaling forty rooms, an orchard, and poultry sheds for five thousand chickens.[25] Up to thirty men could stay at a time, developing skills, work habits, and confidence before returning to the labor force. In return for their efforts, they received room and board, clothes, and a fresh start in life.

Among the many touched by Mother Bird, few became better known than Victor Benke. Hallimond wrote that Benke arrived at the Bowery Mission unable to speak English, with a "huge mop of gnarled and knotted black hair. His face was streaked and caked with dirt, and covered with a beard of many months' growth."[26]

A chance confrontation on a park bench brought Benke to the Mission. He came to Tompkins Square Park early one morning, after spending Saturday night in a lumberyard by the East River. But when he sat down, he woke another immigrant already hunched on the bench. This individual, Fritz, had just been rousted from Shinbone Alley by the police, and he was not pleased to be wakened again.

In response to Fritz's profane litany, Benke replied, *"Ich bin müde und hungrig"* (I am tired and hungry). Recognizing his native language – although in a cultured accent – Fritz exclaimed in his own rough German, "Who are you, in heaven's name, and where do you come from?"

"My father was a Pole, my mother was a French-woman, but I was born in Germany and am a German subject," the newcomer said. "My name is Victor Hugo Benke."[27]

Describing the Mission's free food, Fritz led the way to the Bowery chapel, where the two settled in a back pew among other dozing transients. When Mother Bird entered with a cheery greeting, Benke woke to their answering "Good morning!"

The Sunday service consisted of scripture, sermon, and singing. This particular morning, however, the pianist was absent. After trying to lead a hymn, Mother Bird asked, "Can anyone here play piano?"

The congregation erupted at the idea of a musician in their midst. Mother Bird, in her widow's attire, smiled and held her ground. Leaning toward his translator, Benke asked what the laughter was about, and Fritz explained that the lady wanted a pianist.

> All at once Benke seemed transformed. His two great coal-black eyes were aflame with a new light, and shone like two lamps through the dirty and dusty cloud that lay upon his features. With the grimy fingers of one hand he had grasped the torn lapel of Fritz's coat, while with his other hand he held to the bench in front of his, and half raising himself, he was saying, not in a whisper, but in feverish and excited accents that startled all who were near him: *"Ich kann spielen, ich kann spielen"* (I can play).[28]

Mother Bird welcomed Benke forward, while the congregation clamored, "Gee, look at Professor Hobo. Go to it, Roobenstein!"

"We are trying to sing number 216," Mother Bird explained, handing Benke an open hymnal. Although he could not understand, he later said, "She was so kind, and the tones of her voice were so tender that I was at once reminded of my mother."

Despite the other men's mockery, the youth at the piano rubbed his fingers, then brought them down in a resonant chord. Forgetting hunger and fatigue – and the hymnal – he journeyed through his life on those keys. First came songs of his childhood. Next, with martial strains, he relived his term at the Berlin military academy, before plunging into Beethoven, Bach, Mendelssohn, Wagner, and Schubert. The rowdy crowd was now silent, transfixed.

Fritz pushed his way forward and whispered to his countryman, "They want you to play number 216." Returning to the present, Benke played "Rescue the perishing," while everyone stood up to sing. It was a fitting coincidence that Victor Benke encountered this Fanny Crosby song during his first visit to the Mission. In the following years, the two became a team, collaborating to compose hundreds of hymns.

After the service, Mother Bird paid Benke, and he departed with Fritz, who had been promised a job in Newark. The two stopped at a saloon and quickly spent the money. When Fritz went on, the barkeeper offered Benke janitorial work in exchange for room and board. Benke stayed several days, and his talent might have been buried, had he not honored Mother Bird's invitation to the Mission's Thursday service. Thrilled to see him back, she hired him immediately as the Bowery Mission pianist, a position he kept the rest of his life.

As Victor Benke mastered English, he told Mother Bird his story. His father had been mayor of Ratibor, Silesia (now southern Poland, but then in Germany). Theirs was a musical family; every child played an instrument. Victor's eldest brother, Ernest, became cello soloist in Sir Charles Halle's orchestra in Manchester, England. Their mother died, however, and Victor was left in his older sisters' care. Victor rebelled, and his sisters eventually sent him to America in hopes that a new environment would straighten him out. But when he kept writing for more money, their patience ran out, and they left him to find his own way.

When fortunate, Benke found brief jobs in German beer halls. Otherwise he begged, occasionally landing in jail for breaking panhandling laws. He hit his lowest point in Boston, where, after eight weeks on an oyster boat at the promise of ten dollars a week, he was told he had earned nothing and owed forty-two dollars for passage.

As Mother Bird listened, her interest grew. She arranged to take the young man to one of Dwight L. Moody's revivals at Cooper Union. She was late for their rendezvous, so she went on alone. When she arrived, to her surprise, she saw Benke at the piano. Ira Sankey, who usually played, was ill; when attendees had realized a replacement was needed, several had called out that a Bowery boy here was up to it. Moody was so impressed, he asked Benke to be his accompanist on subsequent visits to New York.

The Bowery Mission has always had an organ. Its most famous, a Hall & Labagh, was built in 1870 for Princeton University's Marquand Chapel. It was installed at the

Mission in 1896 and remained until 1975.[29] Benke gave a
recital on this organ every evening, and he modified it so
he could play drum and cymbals with his feet.

Benke took other jobs – he gave music lessons,
and Ira Sankey contracted him to write two hundred
hymns – but he never accepted an offer that would
interfere with his work at the Mission. He managed
the Fulton Street Prayer Meeting from 9 a.m. until 6
p.m. Then he would play organ or piano at the Bowery
Mission till 10 p.m. and compose music during his home
commute to Brooklyn on the elevated train.

Victor Benke died in 1904, survived by a wife and
child, and his funeral was held at the Mission. He lived
only thirty-two years, but his hymns are sung to this day.
Probably the best known, and best loved, is "Just as I am."

Benke's colleague, Fanny Crosby, lived to ninety-five.
Renowned as "the blind poet," she wrote over eight thou-
sand hymns, including familiars like "To God Be the
Glory" and "Blessed Assurance."

Born in 1820 and raised in Brewster, New York,
Crosby spent much of her life on the east coast working
among criminals, prostitutes, and the unemployed. She
first visited the Bowery Mission in 1881, after meeting
Jeremiah McAuley and joining the gospel rescue mission
movement. An anniversary service was held every
November in those years, to commemorate the Mission's

founding. Crosby attended sixteen of these, penning a poem each time.

According to her biographer, Edith Blumhofer, "Crosby's convictions about the brokenness of all humanity made her reject harsh reproofs and judgmental language in her dealings with those whom evangelicals denominated 'lost.'"[30] Her lyrics echoed her attitude:

> Speak not harshly when reproving
> Those from duty's path who stray;
> If you would reclaim the erring,
> Kindness must each action sway.

On Crosby's eighty-fifth birthday in 1905, hundreds of thousands of Christians sang her songs.[31] Louis Klopsch had announced the idea (hatched by New York clergy) to *Christian Herald* readers worldwide, and "Fanny Crosby Sunday was celebrated in remote Tasmania and in other places where missionaries had taken her hymns."[32]

Like Mrs. Ruliffson and Mother Bird, Fanny Crosby died in 1915. The piano at which she composed her music still stands at Number 227 Bowery, a reminder of her dedication.

Perhaps the wealthiest Bowery Mission partner was J. C. Penney. His devout parents were poor, but they raised their son with a strong work ethic, and he quickly became the success his name connotes. Their faith, however, had little impact during his first forty years.

In 1910, Penney's wife caught pneumonia while he was
on a business trip. She died some days later. Distraught,
Penney started roaming New York City's streets. At
the East River, he toyed with thoughts of suicide but
continued to wander, ending up on the Bowery.

This was just months after the Mission had opened
its chapel, and Penney slipped inside. To his surprise,
he found a fellow businessman telling his conversion
story, detailing his downward spiral and describing how
Mission workers had given him hope. This encounter
restored Penney's courage, and he left a charitable
gift – the first of many – as he departed.

In 1926 Penney established the JCPenney Foundation,
hiring Daniel Poling as its head. Poling in turn invited
Penney to become Christian Herald president the
following year. The timing was perfect, because in
1927 the Mission was in fiscal decline. Under Penney's
leadership, the Bowery Mission and its partner ministries
were financially back on track by the time the Great
Depression hit. When the stock market crashed, Penney's
stock plummeted from one hundred and forty dollars to
thirteen dollars per share. Despite facing personal ruin,
he was committed to save the Mission. As journalist
Tony Carnes writes:

> He spent every last cent he had to do so. He took a
> loan out on his life insurance, he closed down his home
> except for a few rooms, his wife canned tomatoes and

fruits. [He had remarried.] He poured everything into
the Mission. Finally, he made the Mission and its associated organizations debt free. He could do no more.
He gave the Christian Herald Association, The Bowery
Mission, and other organizations to Daniel Poling with
the instruction to take care of them.[33]

While Penney was instrumental in restoring the
Mission's economic security, the Mission played a significant role in his spiritual journey from businessman to
philanthropist to believer. He continued to invest in the
Mission – and minister there – until the end of his life.
He led at least one man to faith, at a chapel service. And
the Bowery Mission has continued its relationship with
the JCPenney Foundation for more than a century.

Superintendent John Hallimond died of a heart attack in
1924 at his cottage in Belmar, New Jersey. He "left prac-
tically no estate, having given all he had to the rescue
work."[34] He had led for twenty-five years and one day.

Another memorable superintendent, a Mississippi
Baptist named Charles Jackson St. John, held the post for
a decade, starting in 1931. Charismatic, even bombastic,
he was also genuinely sympathetic. As one acquain-
tance described him, "God gave him the physique of
a prizefighter and the heart of the good Samaritan."[35]
Where Methodist John Hallimond had developed social
programs, St. John focused on personal salvation. He

preached across denominations in churches throughout the country, hosted a popular radio show, and wrote a book titled *God on the Bowery*.

Charles St. John was the third of seven sons. Describing his family, he wrote, "There was a Bible-reading dad and a praying mother and a sense of nearness of God and a way of living that Jesus of Nazareth would call good."[36] At Mississippi College, he was a center in football, third baseman on the baseball team, junior class president, and editor of *The Mississippi College Magazine* business section. A popular student with a rebellious streak, he took to drinking and was often in trouble. Nevertheless, he began sensing a call to preach. He graduated with a bachelor's degree in 1914.

After serving as a marine during World War I, St. John became a salesman. With his dynamic personality, he was drawn briefly into politics. "I had to keep moving to keep ahead of God's voice,"[37] he later wrote. He had shrunk from the ministry since his college days, drinking fast and hard to escape his vocation.

> Getting drunk with a crowd of "boozem" companions wasn't my style; I took it alone. I'd get a room in a hotel, stock up with enough whiskey to last ten days or two weeks, hang out the "Don't Disturb" sign, lock the door, and go to it. . . . I kept it up for years, losing one job after another, losing every friend I had (except my mother), losing my self-respect, my nerve, my manhood, losing

almost everything but that haunting, pitiless Voice that just wouldn't drown: "St. John, you're going to preach."[38]

Once Charles St. John relented, his transformation was quick and deep. He gave up alcohol, and after his home church licensed him to preach, he enrolled at Southwestern Theological Seminary in Fort Worth, Texas. After seminary, "I caught the fastest train East I could find, and made for the most hopeless mission field in the country – for the Bowery. I was on my feet now, and ready to go."[39]

> Friends drop in on me, once in a while, to ask "Charlie, how do you stand it? How do you stand this endless parade of misery? Day in, day out, always the same!" They say it would drive them crazy. It doesn't drive me crazy. There's more excitement and drama and more of a field for two-fisted religion down here than anywhere else in the world. Day in and day out? No two days are alike, no two hours are alike.[40]

As superintendent, Charles St. John hosted "The Bowery Mission Services," a CBS Radio program broadcast live from the Mission. Featuring testimonials of changed lives, the program also allowed the unemployed to tell their stories – and describe their skills – in hope of getting work. St. John might appeal for funds, clothes, or wheelchairs. Listeners enjoyed this lively show. When one Mission resident went on the air to say his wooden leg had broken, St. John received a call within minutes from a prosthetics manufacturer offering to design a cork leg.

Tommy Dix, the man in his nineties who still recollected the Third Avenue elevated train, also remembered Charles St. John. Known as the "Baritone of the Bowery" in his youth, Dix had been a regular on the radio broadcast. "Rev. St. John was an interesting man, a dynamic personality," Dix told me. "And while he was an imposing figure, he had a strong sense of compassion."

A story in *God on the Bowery* exemplifies Charles St. John's style. One evening a hotel chef came to the door, and the superintendent invited him in. The visitor explained that he had attended a Mission service and noticed that no collection was taken – at which he realized there was probably not a nickel among these men.

"I got kind of ashamed of myself sitting there, thinking how many nickels I had that I threw away on slot machines and cigarettes and movies I forgot as soon as I was out of the theatre." With that, he placed a sack of nickels on Charles St. John's desk, saying, "Take 'em. They're yours. Divide 'em up, and a year from now I'll be back with another bag." Then he left.

Next day at chapel, Charles St. John said:

Fellows, a man left this money with me last night, for you. He's taken an interest in you, and he's willing to bet this bag of nickels that some of you have manhood enough left to straighten up and walk like men again. He gave me these nickels to help me help you do that. I'm going to pass them out, one to each man. I'm not going to ask any questions of you, or demand any promises from you. All I'm asking you to do is to remember that like Christ, this man who has never seen you has a lot of faith in you; all he asks of you is that you invest them the best way you know how. All I ask is that you tell me, six weeks from tonight, what you did with your nickel. You don't even have to do that if you don't want to. It's up to you. Get in line. Come and get it.

Charles St. John describes four of the men who received nickels that night. The first he calls Fred. After graduating from high school, Fred had been unable to find work. When his mother took a scrubwoman's job to continue supporting him, Fred was mortified. He jumped a freight train going west, but he failed to find work in town after town and soon took to stealing food. He was in and out of jails from coast to coast.

After three years, at age nineteen, Fred found himself on the Bowery. He drifted into the Mission the night of the nickels. "I'd made up my mind that night to either get a meal and a bed or go jump in the East River," Fred later told Charles St. John. "If you hadn't been there to take me in the cops would have fished out another body for the morgue."

Clutching his nickel in the Mission dormitory that night, Fred couldn't sleep. Something kept urging him, "Go call your Mother!" Finally he got up, ran to a restaurant, and phoned her. When he heard his mother's voice, he started to weep. All she could say was, "My boy! My boy!" Fred ran back to the Mission, woke the superintendent, and told him what had happened. He begged for a second nickel, for subway fare to see his mother. Suspicious, Charles St. John went along; thus, he witnessed the tearful reunion.

The second nickel went to Hank, a mechanic who had been on the Bowery several months. When he reported back, he said he'd initially meant to panhandle for more and spend the money on liquor. But he told himself, "Hank, it ain't right. It ain't square. Here's a guy who's never seen you, and he bets a nickel on you."

He bought a two-cent newspaper and turned to the classifieds, where his eye was caught by an ad for a mechanic – placed by his former supervisor. Hank spent the remaining three cents on a stamp, wrote his boss a letter, gave the Mission as his address, and waited. The reply came a couple days later: "You don't deserve it, Hank, but I'll give you one more chance just because you're a good mechanic. Report Monday." His second week on the job, Hank got his tools out of the pawn shop and made good.

Here's how Charles St. John reported on the third:

The story of Nickel Number Three is short and not sweet. The man who got it put it in a slot machine, pulled the

lever and found himself rich, just like that. The machine
paid him twenty nickels – a dollar! He got dead drunk
within twenty minutes, woke up in an alley to find a
lush diver making off with his clothes and what was left
of the dollar. He came in the back door of the Mission
and asked for an overcoat and another nickel. He got
the coat, no nickel. He's seventy years old. He'll never
be different. The Mission will forgive him seventy times
seven and someday he'll drop dead in the street or freeze
to death in an alley and we'll bury him. That's that.

When the next man held out his hand for Nickel
Number Four, Charles St. John looked him sharply in the
eye. "Joe, I'll bet a dime you're going to bury this nickel,"
he said. Joe could not sleep, the words repeating in his
mind until, around midnight, they clicked into place: his
dad had told a Bible story about a man burying his talent
in the ground. Joe got thinking how he had buried every
talent he ever had. He decided to do something with this
opportunity.

In the morning, he bought five newspapers at a penny
each. He sold them for two cents apiece, bought ten
more, and sold them. He did the same the next day, and
the next. Noting his determination, the newspaperman
offered him a newsstand. Joe told Charles St. John, "It
isn't much of a stand, as stands go, but it's mine, and I'm
doing a nice little business. Got a good suit now, and the
beginnings of a good account at the saving bank and I'm

paying my own way." As Charles St. John watched Joe at
his newsstand, shouting "Extra! Extra! Read all about
the big battle in Europe!" he wondered if Joe "really
knows what a big battle he's won for himself, on a capital
of five cents."[41]

Rev. George Bolton was superintendent from 1942 until
1959.[42] A strong leader in the rescue mission movement,
he had been president of the International Union of
Gospel Missions for years. He had not always traveled
this road, however.

George Bolton was born in 1899, in Bolton,
England – the Lancashire city that shared his name. As
a teenager during World War I, he served in the Fifty-
Third Battalion of the King's Liverpool Regiment. After
the war, he fell into gambling and drinking. He married,
but later abandoned his wife and three daughters.

Moving across the ocean, Bolton hit the streets of
New York, his life purposeless. One day in 1927, looking
for food, he walked into Jeremiah McAuley's mission.
The message he heard there reached his heart and
changed his life. He determined to spend the rest of it
serving Christ.[43]

After becoming an American citizen and a Presbyterian minister, Bolton plunged into work for the homeless,
eventually finding his place as superintendent at the
Bowery Mission. He often told his own story to give

hope to others struggling with addictions. According to the *New York Times*, Bolton "bridled when anyone called the men in his congregation 'bums.' 'Gentlemen,' he addressed them in his sermons, believing that, with God's help, they could regain a dignity they had lost."[44]

A 1948 newspaper column by Daniel Poling states that George Bolton "does not believe in preaching to empty stomachs and freezing bodies. And he doesn't use food as a trap for his gospel message. He believes that food and the gospel are natural partners, but each stands on its own feet. Whether a man remains to pray, he is fed and clothed."[45] Bolton remained at this post until his death at age sixty, on July 30, 1959.

The Bowery Mission superintendents were a rough-and-ready lot, prepared at any moment to lend a listening ear or break up a fight. They did not mince words, but neither did they condemn anyone beaten down by life. In the 1970s, the superintendent's tasks were split among administrative director, program director, and chapel director. When this last became my responsibility, I placed photos of John Hallimond and Charles St. John above my desk. With their vigilance, empathy, humility, and humor, these forerunners had set the Mission's tone and direction, and the programs they implemented form the core of today's ministry. Using their office behind the chapel balcony – and glancing at their photos – spurs me to serve in the same spirit.

Countless partners have supported the Mission in the century since Mother Bird and Fanny Crosby donated their time and energy. Billy Graham came during a 1957 crusade at which he told his Madison Square Garden audience, "I believe that if Jesus were here today, He would be down there [in the Bowery] much of the time with these people who need Him so much."[46]

About thirty partner churches in the tri-state area regularly lead chapel services. They represent a range of denominations but downplay any differences, keeping God's love foremost. All involved pastors attend an annual retreat at Mont Lawn Camp and gather for a prayer breakfast four times a year.

Three of these churches have sent monthly teams for a hundred years or more. First Baptist Church in the City of New York (where George Washington was baptized) dates back to 1711 and has worked with the Mission almost since its founding. Fifth Avenue Presbyterian is a leader in homeless advocacy; for example, in a 2001 lawsuit against the city, the church successfully defended its right to allow homeless to sleep on its front steps. Calvary Baptist Church brought Billy Sunday in January 1934, and his words were broadcast on NBC Radio. The famed outfielder-turned-evangelist was so energetic, his colleagues had trouble keeping him in front of the microphone. "You talk to those with whom you are daily thrown about the weather, about politics, the NRA and the XYZ – why don't you talk with them about their souls' salvation?" the seventy-one-year-old preacher challenged his listeners. "Where you find one person who resents it you will find ninety-nine who will welcome it."[47]

John Brudermann has preached at chapel every Tuesday morning for nearly thirty years now. He had been an addict for twenty-eight years and a vagrant for six, but he graduated from the Bowery Mission's recovery program in 1984. The day before joining the program, he had a transformational experience that sustained him through his recovery and led him into full-time ministry. Determined to meet people where they were, Pastor John would go into various city parks with a shopping cart of food, which he'd distribute while sharing the gospel with any who would listen. This was the start of the mobile food pantry. As well as several churches, he established the Royal Priesthood Motorcycle Club.

Another partner, Frank Jacobs of the Crossroads Assembly of God in New Jersey, comes once a month. Forty years ago, when Frank asked his fiancée's father for his daughter's hand, the future father-in-law had a request of his own: he needed someone to take his place as volunteer at the Mission. Frank agreed and has ministered faithfully ever since.

Almost every weekend, an a cappella choir of Amish and Mennonites arrive from Pennsylvania, Ohio, and upstate New York. Although they have been coming for more than fifty years, they still turn heads as they stroll past graffiti-littered storefronts and overflowing trash-cans – the women in head coverings and long dresses, the men with bowl haircuts, plain clothes, and suspenders. In her book *Saturday Night,* Susan Orlean describes this unique relationship:

> . . . years ago, an elder of a Mennonite Church in Lancaster, Pennsylvania, was passing through New York and somehow chanced upon the Bowery Mission. Its effort to feed the hungry and save the wretched so impressed him that he determined that when he got back to Pennsylvania he would have his church adopt the Mission as one of its charitable ventures. A ride from Lancaster to the Bowery would cover about two hundred miles and some sociological diversity. Most Mennonites had never taken that ride before this incident, just as most habitués of the mission had never before come into contact with members of this pacifist, agrarian, strict Protestant sect. Nonetheless, the elder's enthusiasm for the place eventually spread from his church to many other Mennonite churches in the Lancaster area, forging a connection between the sect and the Lower East Side of Manhattan that would probably strike many as unlikely. . . [48]

To this day, the Bowery Mission depends on its diverse partners. It could not fulfill its calling without them.

5 Greatheart Chapel

Mr. Wynn is Jamaican. He speaks with a British accent and always wears a suit. Yet often, when he dropped by the Mission to talk with me, his words would be rude and his tattered suit dirty, a result of the crack cocaine and alcohol that ruled his life and stole both his home and his job.

After attending several Bible studies, Mr. Wynn started asking about baptism. I could see that he was serious. When Easter arrived, however – the day appointed for the baptism – he hesitated outside the Mission chapel. I was disappointed, but I knew this was a decision no person can make for another.

Just as the last person was stepping from the water, Mr. Wynn dashed down the aisle, pulling a pipe from his pocket and calling, "Baptize me, baptize me!" Shattering his crack pipe on the altar, he leapt into the pool. His splash further soaked my already wet clothes, but my spirit soared, and I could not suppress my emotion as I asked if he was ready to start a new life and if he believed that God forgave and loved him. "Yes," he declared.

When he stood up, I said, "Mr. Wynn, I better put you in those baptismal waters once more, for good measure."

"Do it, Pastor!" he exclaimed. In the five years since, he has remained free from drugs and alcohol, procured a home, and returned to his former job as an accountant.

The chapel where I baptized Mr. Wynn is called the Greatheart of the Bowery, and it truly is the Mission's heart. Superintendent Hallimond is thought to have named the long hall, after a character in John Bunyan's *Pilgrim's Progress:* "But now Great-Heart replied, 'I am a servant of the God of Heaven; my business is to persuade sinners of repentance. I am commanded to do my endeavor to turn men, women and children, from darkness to light, and from the power of Satan to God.'" Hallimond's second book, published posthumously in 1925, is entitled *The Greatheart of the Bowery.*

In June 2012 the chapel was designated a historic landmark, verifying its place in New York City history.[1] What happens inside is more significant than the building's intriguing background and architecture, however, for it is the spirit in which meals, clothes, clinic, and showers are provided that sets the Bowery Mission apart, and the chapel is often the first touch point for newcomers. Three services per day are held here; it is the most active pulpit in New York City. Yet, while all are invited to join the service, no one is required to attend.

Three times a day, all other Mission activities pause (social work, clothing distribution, and classes) as staff, volunteers, and students gather in the vestibule. Everyone lays one hand on the red doors with a prayer that each soul who enters might encounter the living God. Then the doors are opened, and we focus our communal energy on sharing the gospel. When the worship service ends, our visitors are ushered into Fellowship Hall for a meal.

There is a story behind the chapel's iconic red doors. It starts with a man who caroused in Lower East Side neighborhoods through the 1960s and 70s. His name is Frank Randy, and he failed the Mission's recovery program seventeen times. It took a near-death experience to get his life on course.

Randy had started drinking at fifteen, using alcohol to boost his self-esteem. "My love for that poison cost me a lot of things and took many years from my life," he told me. "It got me kicked out of my family, the army, different jobs, and, eventually, homeless shelters. It was a continuous cycle I just couldn't break out of."

Randy got his meals at the Mission, but he was living on the streets. It wasn't until he was stabbed one night that he got serious about changing his ways. Although he nearly bled to death, he made it to the Mission, where a worker received him and called an ambulance. After treatment, Randy returned. This time – his eighteenth try – he graduated the recovery program, having learned to rely on prayer and hard work instead of liquor. He found a job that he held for the next thirty-seven years. He was married for thirty-nine years. A widower now, retired on Staten Island, he says, "I wouldn't be alive without the Bowery Mission, guaranteed. Luckily God chose to save me, forty years ago, and keeps me around to tell my story."

Randy was the one who painted the chapel doors red, to symbolize Christ's blood as the entrance to life. Ever since, doors at every Bowery Mission location – from the women's centers to Mont Lawn Camp – have been painted red.

Although the Bowery Mission began in 1879, it moved from place to place for thirty years. With the chapel's opening at Number 227, on November 7, 1909, the Mission found its lasting home. John Hallimond had just completed his first decade of leadership at the time, Louis Klopsch was still president of the Christian Herald, and the organization was deeply involved in anti-poverty work.

The Neo-Grec edifice at 227 Bowery had been constructed in 1876 for an undertaker, Jonas Stoltz, as a five-story coffin factory with a mortuary in the basement.[2] Staff are often quick to note that this place, built for death, has been serving life for over a century.

When the Mission first leased the red brick building, architects Marshall and Henry Emery were employed to transform it into an elegant sanctuary with attached dining hall and kitchen.[3] They exposed the chapel's ceiling to reveal its beams and arched trusses, and installed four exceptional Benjamin Sellers stained-glass windows depicting the prodigal son's homecoming.

The 1898 blaze that had destroyed Number 105 motivated Mission organizers to make Number 227 as fireproof as possible.[4] Floors were rebuilt of steel and concrete, overlaid with tile. Any wood was covered to the ceiling with stonework, door and window frames were covered with metal,[5] and the speaker's platform was made of marble.

The chapel aesthetics and design would remain virtually unaltered for the next 110 years, until a 2018 reconfiguration replaced the history-rich pulpit, pews, and preachers' chairs with a portable stage, interlocking plastic chairs, and two large projection screens.

Under the auspices of the Christian Herald, the Mission purchased Number 227 outright in 1928. When the building was designated a historic site in 2012, the Landmark Commission stated: "Number 227 Bowery is significant for its 103-year history as the home of the Bowery Mission, a religious-based organization that has fed, housed, and cared for countless homeless men on the Lower East Side for more than 130 years."

Those who meet regularly in the chapel – and those who
work here – are in many ways like family. We laugh and
we cry, we share stories and memories, and we sometimes
disappoint each other. Fred, a former maintenance man,
recalls, "One summer my assistant secretly cut all the
heating pipes out of the basement. When I was certain
who had done it, another staff member and I confronted
the guy, who admitted to taking the pipes and selling the
copper to support a heroin relapse. He was then assigned
to help me re-plumb the basement, a mammoth task."

At the Mission, we have special traditions and rites
that affirm our sense of community: baptisms, funerals,
marriages, dedications, and foot washing.

Performing the foot-washing service, each Easter
Thursday, is humbling. It is also humbling for our guests
to receive. Yet dozens come forward, removing dirty
footwear to allow their calloused and sometimes disfig-
ured feet to be bathed, while a volunteer plays the piano
and another reads the Gospel account of Jesus washing
his disciples' feet. My coworkers and I bring towels,
washcloths, and clean socks, and we refill the tub for
each person.

The smell is not pleasant when homeless people take
off their shoes. But our guests sit on ornate handcrafted
furniture. When elderly Burtham shuffled forward,
I told him, "Sit back and relax like royalty, brother."

Looking up while tending his weary feet, I saw him as King Burtham, regal and dignified.

As I dried one man's feet, I realized he was weeping. My eyes met his, and he falteringly voiced his feelings. He had lost count of the years that people had avoided him, he said. Now another human being had reached out and touched him, in love.

There were no documented baptisms at the Mission until recent years, and there is no built-in pool, but we hold a baptism each Easter Sunday. We used to use the Chinese Evangel Mission Church, going there by van after our 7 a.m. Bowery service and returning to the Mission for breakfast after the baptism. But in 2014 – the year Mr. Wynn was baptized – we purchased an inflatable pool.

In 1913 James Hunt, then secretary of the Bowery Mission, dedicated his one-year-old son, Jimmy Hunt Jr., in the Greatheart.[6] The child's mother had recently died. Bowery Mission staff have always supported one another; twenty-one godfathers and godmothers came to stand with the Hunts, father and son.

Superintendent Hallimond officiated. "Do you declare, in the hearing of Almighty God and in the presence of this congregation that it is your true, sincere, and solemn desire and determination to dedicate this child to the service of God and his fellow-men?"

"I do," the father replied.

Turning to the godparents, Hallimond said, "I call upon you, brethren and sisters, fellow workers with Brother Hunt in the Bowery Mission, to be witnesses to this his solemn act of dedication, and those of you who are willing and prepared by your prayers, sympathy, and influence to aid him in his purpose of training this child for active service in the cause of lost humanity, please signify it by raising your right hand." The twenty-one raised their hands. (A letter from President Woodrow Wilson, commemorating the Mission's thirty-fourth anniversary, was read aloud on the same occasion.)

The next recorded dedication took place a century later, at a Friday night jazz service in 2013, when my wife and I brought our son, Elgin, to the Greatheart. We chose this place because Jesus identified with the poor; we believed he would be closest here. Family members, Mission workers, Mennonite bishops and ministers, and nearly two hundred homeless men and women attended, as Kenn Thompson, a ministry partner, officiated Elgin's dedication.

The first documented communion service did not take place until the early 2000s. Reggie Stutzman, chapel director at the time, says he was feeling "quite religious" while setting out the grape juice and wafers – when a homeless man entered the chapel. He had soiled himself and smelled accordingly. Reggie left his preparations to help the newcomer get a shower and clean clothes. The service took place as planned. Later, however, Reggie said that in caring for the vagrant he experienced deeper communion with God than he did in the ritual.

Marriages have also been a part of the Bowery Mission's story. In 1911, Anna Butler, a young volunteer from a wealthy Massachusetts home, married her first convert, "Sunny Jim" Kronenberg. While Anna was refined and petite, burly Sunny Jim, forty-five, was over six feet tall. They had found each other at the Mission, but their ceremony took place at Hadley Rescue Hall. His rowdy acquaintances joined her cultured family and friends to celebrate the wedding.[7]

While other Bowery romances led to marriage, there were no weddings in the Greatheart until 1969. On August 3 that year the *New York Times* reported, "A minister who became a drunkard and then reformed was married yesterday in the first wedding ever performed at the Bowery Mission in its 90 years of trying to salvage human derelicts."[8] Superintendent John Lockwood solemnized the marriage; the groom, James Carter, had assisted him for two years.

The story became a sensation days later, when a letter to the *Times* declared that Carter's claim – of being an Episcopalian priest who turned to alcohol after his first wife died in childbirth – was false. The *Times* ran a follow-up article, "Bowery Worker Posed as Cleric," in which Carter confessed that he had fabricated the story to rouse sympathy. Daniel Poling stood by Carter, telling the *Times*, "We want Jim to continue at his job in the mission. We can't let a good man go." Carter's bride stood by him too, saying, "I love Jim as much as ever – even more now. He's going to do a great job for God."[9]

Other weddings have taken place in the Greatheart over the years. Diamond and Michael exchanged their vows here in September 2011. They had first met in the chapel, during volunteer orientation, and Michael later proposed to her at the same spot. They invited homeless people as their guests, inspired by the wedding banquet parable.

Charles and Cheryl Reaves were married here in 2013. They had been together more than twenty years, but had not gotten married earlier due to his addiction.

At age fifteen, Charles had run away from home and gotten into drugs. As he wandered down the Bowery, someone called, "Hey kid, you look hungry," inviting him into the Mission for a meal. Since Charles was underage, workers then phoned his mother, who took him home.[10]

Trying to straighten out, Charles enrolled in the Job Corps. He became bitter, however, when one of his friends was murdered. He joined the National Guard and entered a relationship with Cheryl, but his drug addiction still consumed him. After many years, he remembered and returned to the Bowery Mission. Begging God to remove his desire for drugs, he entered the recovery program. On its completion, he proposed to Cheryl. I counseled the couple for two months before officiating their marriage. Cheryl has recently finished nursing school. Charles, who remains active in the Mission's alumni program, became a carpenter. He has remained drug-free.

Funerals, too, have taken place in the Greatheart, for many destitute and for several staff, including Superintendent Hallimond, whose body lay in repose in the Mission chapel. The *New York Times* reported, "For the six hours a stream of men poured in from the Bowery, many of them ragged and unkempt, to pay their last respects to the superintendent. Hundreds of them knelt beside the coffin and wept."[11]

Reggie Stutzman held several funerals during his tenure at the Mission. His first was for Don Howard, whom he described to me as "a crusty old man with a mean disposition, but he was part of the community." When Howard disappeared for weeks, Reggie called the Bellevue morgue. The chief medical examiner told him Howard had died on a train, surrounded by empty beer cans. The morgue planned to send the body to Potter's Field, the city's cemetery for unidentified and unclaimed bodies, but a transgender prostitute informed

Reggie that Catholic Charities had benevolent lots. For
five hundred dollars, a funeral home near Union Square
put Howard in a pine box, brought him to the Mission,
and buried him in Woodlawn Cemetery. Reggie did the
eulogy, and ministry partners donated flowers.

Reggie's second memorial service was for a young man
known only as "Jimmy," who died outside the Mission
during a seizure. Since his identity was unknown,
Catholic Charities again provided a Woodlawn plot.
Weeks later, however, an investigator turned up saying
that Jimmy's parents had hired him to search for their
missing son. Reggie told him all he knew. Being Jewish,
the family exhumed Jimmy's body to rebury in their
own cemetery. But his mother called to tell Reggie how
vivacious her son had been before being hooked by
heroin – and to express her gratitude to the Mission for
preventing his burial in a pauper's grave.

I, too, have led funerals. Andre Griffin's was one.
When I arrived, he had been around longer than any
staff member, a regular fixture at the Mission. Born in
Puerto Rico in 1945, he served with the United States
Army from 1966 to '68. He landed on the Bowery, a war
zone of its own, soon after returning from Vietnam.

Andre drank heavily, and when he was sixty-eight, his
organs began shutting down. He rapidly lost weight, and
one day in the chapel he fell into a coma – in his personal
spot, the second-to-last pew. An ambulance took him

to Beth Israel Hospital, and several of his friends joined me there to hold his hands and pray over him. When he died a few days later, I claimed the body, since he had no family. He was honored at a gathering attended by staff, students, and a host of homeless men and women.

As a veteran, Andre was eligible for a plot at Calverton National Cemetery, and the Army Honor Guard played taps and folded the flag. His headstone inscription reads, "A friend of The Bowery Mission. Luke 6:20." He had been with us so long, his death seemed the end of an era.

Barry Stage was one of the men who visited Andre in the hospital. Barry was a gentle soul, but obviously homeless, and nurses refused to admit him until I arrived and confirmed that he was Andre's friend.

Barry had been drifting for more than thirty years when a Mission social worker found him an apartment. Unfortunately, he learned he had cancer even before moving in, and he lived there less than a year. Shortly before his death, Barry discovered that he was entitled to full military benefits – even though he had been discharged from the army after just a few weeks in boot camp. He was buried in the same cemetery as Andre and given the same inscription.

Since homeless people have to struggle so hard for what most take for granted, they are doubly challenged when storms or calamities strike. At such times, the Greatheart

Chapel is a literal sanctuary – from blizzard, hurricane, personal trouble, or national disaster.

Reggie Stutzman had been chapel director for less than a month in September 2001. While commuting to work on Tuesday, the eleventh, he noticed smoke coming from the north tower of the World Trade Center. The Mission was undergoing renovations, and when Reggie arrived, he saw a businessman leaning on the scaffolding, sobbing, "I have never been late in my entire career, but this morning I was!" The man's tardiness had saved his life. And his workplace, just a mile and a half from 227 Bowery, would soon be a smoldering mountain of rubble.

Throughout that day, Reggie stood in the street, calling, "Water and bathrooms!" as more than a thousand soot- and ash-smeared escapees arrived at the chapel's oasis. Some collapsed in shock. The kitchen kept steadily producing soup and sandwiches.

A decade later, Hurricane Sandy disrupted the eastern seaboard. Lives were lost, damage mounted into billions of dollars, and storm surges devastated New York City. With no electric power, Manhattan went dark. Police stationed themselves on key corners to prevent looting or riots. But while the "haves" departed for safe places of light, running water, and Wi-Fi, the "have-nots" stayed behind in the chaos.

While many city shelters shut down, the Bowery Mission remained open. I watched as masses of people arrived, in search of hot food and a working toilet or huddling together for warmth. We ran floodlights from generators. With no sound system, I stood in the middle of the chapel and shouted out the story of Jonah, emphasizing his prayer of faith when there was nowhere to go and life seemed over.

Early the next morning – when the Greatheart chapel was still dark, and I could barely make out silhouettes, let alone faces – I announced that we would distribute clothes and hoped to soon provide showers (albeit cold ones). We could do little, but I suggested that we pray. From the darkness, individuals began shouting out requests. Each time the community responded in unison, "Lord, hear our prayer."

"Lord, turn on the lights!" called a voice.

"Lord, hear our prayer," responded a couple hundred more.

"Let me fix my messed-up life!"

"Lord hear our prayer."

"We need showers today!"

"Lord, hear our prayer."

"Help me get a job."

"I want to be back with my wife and kids."

"Give me an apartment."

"Thank you for this safe place to sleep!"

I closed the prayer meeting by thanking God for hearing all our spoken and unspoken yearnings. By afternoon, we were able to meet everyone's basic needs. Gradually, over the next weeks, the Mission returned to normal.

Normal, at the Mission, is responding to a steady stream of more personal tragedy. At 7 p.m. one Thanksgiving Day, a woman entered the chapel, crying and cursing. When asked for her name, she snapped that she was Jessica and that her plastic bag contained everything she owned. While a staff member fetched hot food and drink, teenage volunteers rallied to encourage Jessica. I had to lead the chapel's eleventh (and final) service of the day, then help serve another two hundred Thanksgiving meals, so it was a long time before I returned.

When I did, Jessica was laughing, showing photos of her kids to the volunteers. A Mission worker offered to take her to a drop-in shelter, and I heard Jessica tearfully thank the teenagers as she left, still clutching her bag. Meanwhile, I could see perhaps a hundred men moving pews from the holiday tent back into the Greatheart – where the gospel is preached, where dozens of men find a place to sleep, and where this lady who had arrived in tears of rage was leaving in tears of gratitude.

Today the Mission operates programs for men, women, and children throughout New York City and beyond, but its heart remains Number 227 Bowery.

6   On the Frontline

We often see an increase in illegal activity along the Bowery in June, July, and August; with crowds on the street, the underground economy thrives. Carlo and Sharif were both in their twenties the summer that someone warned me they were pedaling dope outside the Mission. Carlo had failed our program twice, due to anger issues. Sharif is schizophrenic.

Watchful, I soon realized these young men were indeed selling heroin and a barbiturate known as sticks. I searched the Mission's crannies for paraphernalia and discovered a bag of needles, swabs, and tie-ups stashed between scaffolding.

Seeing me confiscate the goods, Carlo charged me. It was just him and me at that moment, and we circled each other for a minute that felt like forever. A crowd of homeless men was starting to gather, and thankfully Carlo backed down. I threw the bag in the trash, and I announced at chapel that anyone buying or selling drugs near the Mission would be denied services.

The two were furious, and fellow staff offered to escort me home. I reasoned, however, that I'm in the wrong field if I need protection from the people I serve, so I departed alone as usual. I saw Sharif when I turned the corner onto Stanton Street. He was crossing toward me, brandishing a baseball bat. Then I realized Carlo was sneaking up from behind, knife in hand. I whirled to face him.

Carlo started cursing. He and Sharif knew my commitment to nonviolence, and they were clearly trying to provoke a fight. I declared that I would not tolerate drug sales at the Bowery Mission, no matter what they did to me. Their shouting got louder. Carlo came at me.

Stanton, between Bowery and Chrystie, is a shaded street of private residences and businesses. Hearing the uproar, people started peering through windows or leaning out business doors. The sight of these onlookers probably saved me. Carlo spat in my face, turned, and ran. Sharif, on his heels, paused to fling the bat in my direction.

Next day at chapel, I declared that we who follow Christ are a renewed, forgiven people – released from guilt, bitterness, despair, or anything else that separated us from God. And when we are forgiven, we also forgive others, even debtors and enemies.[1]

Word spread that all Sharif and Carlo had to do was confess and stop dealing, and pardon would be theirs. For the next couple days, however, they kept passing the Mission to shout obscenities. Then they quit coming.

The following week, I heard Carlo call my name as I passed through Chrystie Park on my way home. I stopped to listen. He was apologizing. I told him I forgave him – but that there would still be consequences: he could not return to the Mission until winter, and if he continued to pedal dope on the Bowery he might never be allowed back. He nodded and went his way but turned back to call, "I love you, pastor!" A few days later, Sharif followed suit. To my knowledge, neither has since sold drugs at the Bowery Mission.

The first time a Mission worker is spat on, we call it the "Bowery baptism." And we've all been punched, cursed, or threatened at some point. We are not fighting against people, however. We battle "against the cosmic powers of this present darkness, against the spiritual forces of evil."[2] We certainly experience defeats and setbacks. But our faith is in Christ, who already conquered the enemy, and we, too, experience victories.

Substance abuse is chief among our foes. Addiction propels too many women and men toward prison, destitution, or worse. Jane was seven months pregnant when she and her boyfriend, Jesse, began visiting the Mission. She was young and beautiful but hooked on cocaine and heroin. He had been tall and handsome before a gunfight crippled him, landing him in a wheelchair. After some weeks, the pair stopped coming. I wondered about them until, months later, Jesse dropped by. He was drunk and didn't want to talk, telling me only that Jane had died of an overdose, in police custody, after giving birth to a daughter.

Danger, a Bloods gang member, was another dope fiend. One day I caught him pedaling in front of the Mission. "What are you doing?" I challenged him. "You don't crap where you eat! I don't want you dealing drugs anywhere – but to do it here shows you don't care two cents about this community. Or about yourself!"

Danger mostly stayed away after this confrontation, but occasionally he would be back on the corner – a safe enough distance, he argued – to ply his wares. He eventually succumbed to the dope he was slinging and became a full-on addict. After he attacked one of our volunteers, we had to restrict him from receiving Mission services.

The Bloods warred with a rival gang, Dominicans Don't Play. After Danger attacked Tito, a DDP member with a broken leg – beating Tito with his own crutch and stealing the dope hidden in his cast – fear of Danger spread on the street.

Then one spring day, after lunch cleanup, a colleague and I walked to a local coffee spot on Mott Street to enjoy a drink and pick up a coffee bean donation. As we returned toward the Mission with our load, Danger suddenly appeared with one of his cronies.

Yelling, "I'm going to kill you," he attacked me. I turned the other cheek, as Jesus commanded his followers, but I soon ran out of cheeks and realized I had better defend myself – no easy choice for a pacifist Mennonite. I hit Danger hard, three times, and he fell to the ground. Police arrived to arrest him and his buddy.

Danger was back at the Mission a few days later, this time with two pit bulls and a cohort claiming to belong to the Bloods. Thankfully Miles, a former Bloods gang member, knew about the fight – everyone knew about the fight – and he told Danger and the others they had no cause to attack a pastor, especially one who had helped each of them with anything from clothes to prayer requests. Ashamed, the group dispersed – fortunately for me.

Matthew's problem was alcohol. As soon as he was released after six months in jail – for threatening our deskman with a screwdriver – he went straight to the liquor store and then to the Bowery, where he smashed a bottle against the Mission door and then broke his way in, cutting his hand in the process. Once inside, he tried to attack two staff members. I arrived just then, and we managed to calm him down. Someone had called the cops as soon as Matthew appeared. By the time they reached the scene and took Matthew to Beth Israel Hospital, my arms were red with blood, most of it Matthew's.

This spiritual battle has been waged at the Mission for one hundred and forty years, and the Bible is our inspiration. Despite disappointments and defeats, we repeatedly see captives set free, the oppressed liberated, the sick healed, and those considered intransigent saved by God's grace. Just as a soldier learns to keep low in the trenches, however, so too must Christians remain humble. If we stand up to struggle or strategize in our own strength, all our efforts will fail.

But the Bible is more than a manual for spiritual warfare. Jesus said, "I have come to bring good news to the poor." Therefore, we who proclaim the gospel must address people's physical as well as spiritual needs. All the Bowery Mission's endeavors, from Hallimond's Brotherhood and Winner's Club to our current recovery program, have been guided by Jesus' words: "I was hungry and you gave me food, I was thirsty and you gave me something to drink, I was a stranger and you welcomed me, I was naked and you gave me clothing, I was sick and you took care of me, I was in prison and you visited me. . . . Truly I tell you, just as you did it to one of the least of these who are members of my family, you did it to me."[3]

I was hungry and thirsty . . .

"Serve like you're serving a king" is the motto displayed in our serving line. It's a good reminder, because conflicts tend to erupt while guests are waiting in line for food. The Mission prepares an average of two hundred free meals, three times a day. Our guests do not have to sign in, nor must they attend the chapel service preceding each meal.

As we dish up breakfast, lunch, or dinner, we build relationships with regulars like Ron and Rosa, who are in their second stint on the street. They have been married twenty years and have no drug or alcohol issues – just bad luck, no work, and no health insurance for their medical challenges.

I was a stranger . . .

The Bowery community consists of strangers, including those who are mentally ill, prostitutes, immigrants (documented and undocumented), abusers and abused, alcoholics and addicts. Most feel rejected wherever they go. Many live with guilt. But all are welcome at the Mission.

Yuri and Anna hailed from Greenpoint, a hub of Russian and Polish immigrants. They clearly loved each other but seemed unable to straighten out their lives. Anna, the more dominant one, instigated fights in the chapel, while Yuri followed her around, seemingly disoriented. Then Anna was arrested for shoplifting. While she was in jail, Yuri went to detox to resolve his drug problem. Soon after, though, he was found dead in a Chinatown restaurant bathroom, a heroin needle still stuck in his arm. Anna heard the news in jail. She grieved Yuri's death. Yet after her release, she walked off with another young man whose eyes were drowsy with dope.

Delon Ali was raised in Trinidad by a Muslim father and Hindu mother. After immigrating to the United

States, Ali landed a good job at an upscale Soho retail store, got his own place, and bought a car. But when he began shooting dope, his life spun out of control. Always seeking that next high, he lost his job and apartment and started sleeping on rooftops or in abandoned buildings and subway trains. In his dejection, he isolated himself, seldom bathed, and slashed his wrists numerous times.

Ali heard about the Mission from someone he got high with, and he arrived one frigid winter night seeking emergency shelter. After sleeping on a floor mat, he attended the morning chapel service and joined the recovery program. Dealing with his addictions – and letting go of anger, bitterness, and pride – were challenging for Ali, and he left us after relapsing into drug use. He was ashamed of his failure, but he couldn't seem to cut loose.

Some months later, however, Ali returned for a fresh try, and in 2008 he successfully completed the program. His experience positioned him to help new residents. "Some days they will feel like they cannot keep walking, and that's when you lift them up and encourage them," he says. "Healing is a process. I may have been on my way for several years, but I still don't have it all figured out."

After serving at the Mission, Ali earned an associate degree, followed by a bachelor's; he is now in seminary. He has shared his testimony with news outlets from the *New York Press* to the *Katie Couric Show*, where he reached over a million viewers. Although he spoke throughout the country – in megachurches, small storefront churches, and everything in between – he continued to lead many a morning chapel service at the Mission until he left the United States in 2018.

I was naked . . .

In the dead of winter, we may find a barefoot man or woman at the door. Some people have left the hospital wearing only a flimsy gown. Others soil themselves and arrive reeking. In such instances, we sidestep our schedule of clothing give-out and shower days to meet the need. In addition, once a week we provide interview suits for men referred to us by other agencies. (We send any women needing clothes or showers to McAuley Center on Lafayette Street.)

Jerry, the guest with Tourette Syndrome I mentioned earlier, compulsively rips his clothes and footwear, and he depends on the Mission to provide replacements. This can be difficult, as he is a big man. Fortunately, wives of professional basketball players (New York Knicks and Brooklyn Nets) donate top-of-the-line sneakers every couple of months. Mission staff hold any size 15 or larger for Jerry.

I was sick . . .

There is a saying that the Bowery is where you go to die, so perhaps it is unsurprising that we call an ambulance about once a day. But I never get used to it. The homeless are prone to tuberculosis, HIV, diabetes, seizures, and more. Some have swollen legs, due to poor diet and bad circulation. Then there are all the complications connected with substance abuse. Yet at the Mission, many people gain a new lease on life through faith and proper medical care. In the clinics that we run throughout the week, volunteer doctors, nurses, and social workers adapt advancements in wellness and mental health to meet our clients' needs.

Although I had often witnessed spiritual healing at the Mission – souls freed from addiction, marriages restored, the dispossessed finding homes – I had never seen miraculous physical healing until the day Lori danced into the chapel. A year earlier, under the influence of alcohol, she had stepped into traffic and been hit by a car. She was unable to walk for months. When she finally did, she had a bad limp. One morning I came across Lori on a side street in Alphabet City. Passed out drunk, she was filthy and smelled like feces. I woke her, offered to call an ambulance (which she refused), and prayed for her. When she danced into the Mission weeks later, she told me that after our prayer in Alphabet City, she lost any desire for drink and found she could walk normally. I was awed by God's power.

I was in prison . . .

Red tells me that even in jail he is called a bum, by inmates who recognize him from the streets. The

Mission often gets letters from Bowery men serving time, some of them creating positive plans for their release. Staff members visit them at The Tombs, Riker's Island, Sing Sing, or other prisons in the metropolitan area.

Men in prison uniform have turned up at the door since the Mission first opened. Back when Charles St. John was superintendent, he described "one who came to me in a suit of prison-made clothes. I can spot those prison suits a mile away. They stick out like a neon sign, and to the man who wears one, it is a sign; he knows it is a 'jailbird suit,' and he thinks everybody else knows it, so the first thing we do with him is to get him out of it and into a 'civilian' garment."[4]

I, too, have welcomed men in prison garb. One such ex-offender is now a graduate student at Hunter College. He's pursuing a social work degree to enable him to help others.

Rubén, a Puerto Rican of African descent, told how he came to the Bowery Mission after prison:

Shortly after high school, I went to prison for ten years, and although I was a very tough person on the outside, I would cry a lot at night to God. In the back of my head I knew that ultimately he was the only one who could get me out. On the day I was released from prison the chaplain stood at the doorway – he is a good man – and all he said to me was, "Seek Christians." I wanted to tell him that what I really needed was money, but his comment

stuck with me, and I thought a lot about it on my bus
ride down to the city.

Very quickly I was back onto drugs, and I got real
worried, because I knew I would end up in jail again.
I knew I would die in jail or get killed on the street. I
was kind of down at that point. You know, all my hurts
and pains, physically and psychologically and spiritually, were a cry to God, a form of prayer. I knew I had to
stop using drugs, but that doesn't mean I gave up selling
them (the money was too good). One day I was hanging
around in the streets on the Lower East Side, drinking,
looking at all the money and the weapons, and I said
to myself, "Dear God, I've gotta stop this!" And then I
turned to my buddies and said, "You guys, I'm giving all
this up." I just knew that I had to change.

I decided to go into a rehab program, but everywhere
I went they turned me down; no one wanted to take me.
Then I met a guy called Larry who told me to come to
the Bowery Mission. He told me all about it. I told him
I was not a Christian, and he said that didn't matter. He
told me, "If you are on this corner tomorrow that means
you want to give it a try." So I was there on the corner the
next day.

My time at the Bowery Mission was just a first step,
"basic training," but it was the turning point I needed.[5]

Just as we who work at the Mission take inspiration
from the Bible, so do our guests. In a world that excludes
them, many are thrilled to read, "Do not exploit the

poor because they are poor and do not crush the needy in court, for the Lord will take up their case and will exact life for life."[6] Jesus' mother also exclaimed, "He has brought down the high and mighty from their thrones but has lifted up the poor and those of a humble estate. He has filled the hungry with good things but has sent the rich away empty."[7] These are encouraging words when you're at the bottom.

Biblical prophets grappled with rejection and despair. Jeremiah wished he had never been born.[8] Moses wanted to die at one point,[9] as did Elijah.[10] Amos roared God's rage.[11] Scripture also describes mighty men and women who fell far but found their footing again. Hagar, rejected by her child's father, is cast into the wilderness where she meets God and names him "The one who sees me."[12] And King David's cry, "A broken and contrite heart God will not despise,"[13] was wrung from his soul after shameful failure. Such expressions of remorse are cathartic on the Bowery.

Larry Mason, the one who invited Rubén to the Mission, said, "If you could summarize my old life, it would be like a full garbage can where you kept the lid on real tight." He spelled it out:

> I was born in 1943, and moved to New York City when I was four years old. I only remember seeing my dad once. I never knew the man. To this day, I could walk into my father in the middle of the street and not know him. I

never tried to meet him. It's not that I had hard feelings against him, or my mom. They did what they did, for whatever reason, and that was it. Some things in life we may never know the full reason.

Larry ran away from home, and spent his childhood between the street and state institutions, where he suffered physical, psychological, and sexual abuse. He never completed grade school, and only lasted three days in high school before being thrown out. By age thirteen his life consisted mainly of crime, drugs, and drug dealing. When he was seventeen, his girlfriend got pregnant. They married and had kids, but that didn't last long. Larry continues:

In 1967, I went into the Army. I served in Vietnam, in the First Cavalry Gary Owen Division, from 1968 to '72. I was a "grunt," but I was a good soldier, good at what I did. I killed, and I saw many friends die. One guy, all that was left to send home was his boots. I got caught up in the war spirit, and I kept re-enlisting until they told me, "You've had enough, go home." But I had no real home. Normal society had nothing to offer me anymore.

So I did what I knew best. I set up camp in the bush on Staten Island with a bunch of other guys. Just like in Vietnam, we had a perimeter set up at night, and no one went anywhere without a weapon. I survived as a dealer, until I was arrested in 1977 for robbery and attempted murder. I did three years out of a ten-year sentence, most of it in Attica. I got out in 1981.

After prison Larry found himself right back where he had left off, and knew it was only a matter of time before he was dead. The only alternative he could see was to go back to jail. So he went to the parole office.

> My parole officer was out, so I met with this senior parole officer. He was a Jewish guy. I told him to lock me up again. And to give him a reason, I took out my pistol and laid it on his desk.
>
> This guy reached up, grabbed this pamphlet, and said, "Did you ever hear of the Bowery Mission?" Who hasn't on the street – that's where the bums go, man! But this guy held the keys to my life in his hands. He said, "Larry, why don't you just go down there. You might find what you're looking for."
>
> I remember thinking, "Actually this guy doesn't even have to let me out of this office – he could just handcuff me and take me away."
>
> I was still skeptical, but I decided to give it a chance. He gave me money for the taxi, which I used for a bottle of wine; then I walked on down toward the Mission. I was going down Fifth Avenue, and I stopped in a church. The main sanctuary was closed, so I went into this little chapel. I don't remember if anyone was in there or how long I stayed, but I just started talking to God.
>
> "Look, God," I says, "I'll tell you what I'll do. I have made a lot of deals with the devil, I have danced with the devil, and I never came out a winner. But if you can take my life and you can do something with it, I will give you what's left."

If that's what you promise God, you better mean it. Something happened to me in that church. Sitting there, I wept tears of pain for the first time since I was a kid. I left the chapel, and I felt something. I felt like this weight had been taken – the sun was brighter, the air was clear – but I couldn't put my finger on it. Then I went down to the Bowery Mission.

At the Mission, one of the requirements for newcomers was to go to three chapel services a day for the first thirty days. Pastors came in to lead services, or Wall Street businessmen would use their lunch hour to give a testimony or sing. One day Larry heard someone called Louie giving his testimony.

His story was totally parallel to mine. It was like me talking, but it was coming out of his mouth. He kept referring to Jesus as his running partner. On the street, nothing can come between you and your running partner. It was so personal, it was like he really knew Jesus. So I sat there and I listened – really listened – and I took in what he was saying. Then I realized what actually happened back in that little church: that God had heard my prayer and answered my prayer. Louie prayed with me that night.

Larry ended up staying at the mission for seven years. There, he met volunteers from the Bruderhof, and when he felt the need to move on, he ended up at the Woodcrest Bruderhof, in upstate New York. After some time, he was baptized and became a member.

I have it on my heart that many like me, still out there,
can find what I have found. There is hope beyond
despair! So many Vietnam vets commit suicide or are
living on the streets. All my fellow brothers and sisters,
there is a place where you can find hope, healing, and a
new purpose in life.[14]

Indeed, many veterans – from the Civil War, both World
Wars, Korea, Vietnam, Iraq, and Afghanistan – have
found new life at the Bowery Mission.

Chris is a Desert Storm veteran who had a dramatic
conversion at the Mission. A platoon commander, he was
one of the first to enter urban Baghdad, and he told me
that he vomited the first time he killed an enemy soldier.
This reaction repeated for the first seven. After that,
Chris said, it became "as easy as shooting rabbits."

He was soon called back to Germany, but memories
haunted him. Then he received news from New York
that his twenty-seven-year-old son had been murdered.
Chris flew home for court proceedings. When permitted
to address his son's killer, Chris said he harbored no
vengeful feelings, because he himself had committed
similar atrocities. His words so horrified his wife that she
separated from him.

Chris started using crack and attempted suicide twice.
The first time, he jumped from the Brooklyn Bridge
into the East River, but someone rescued him. The next
time, he dropped onto the FDR Parkway from an over-
pass. Again he survived, but he broke his back. After

rehabilitation in a VA hospital, he continued his crack habit, which brought him to homelessness in fifteen years.

One day in spring 2009 Chris came to the Bowery, intending to buy drugs from a guy known as D-block after lunch at the Mission. Chris entered the red doors, planning to sit through chapel and await the end of lunch. Something hit his heart during the service, however. He found himself in tears, responding to the altar call almost against his will. He knelt at the front, received prayer, and suddenly felt a peace and joy that drove out any desire for crack.

Chris entered the discipleship program. In the following days, he talked endlessly about his experiences to anyone who would listen – his way of confessing his sins. He became a helpful member of the Mission family, encouraging other residents with humor and sensitivity.

One day, Chris saw D-block outside. He went out to greet him, saying, "D-block, I thank you from the bottom of my heart!"

D-block snorted. "What the hell are you talking about!"

"You brought me to Jesus!" Chris replied.

Distressingly, the lure of drugs is never far in the city, tugging whenever someone feels low. Recidivism is a constant danger. Years after Chris's conversion, I learned he was doing drugs again. But as long as they live, I never give up hope for any of my brothers and sisters on the street.

7 Twenty-First-Century Mission

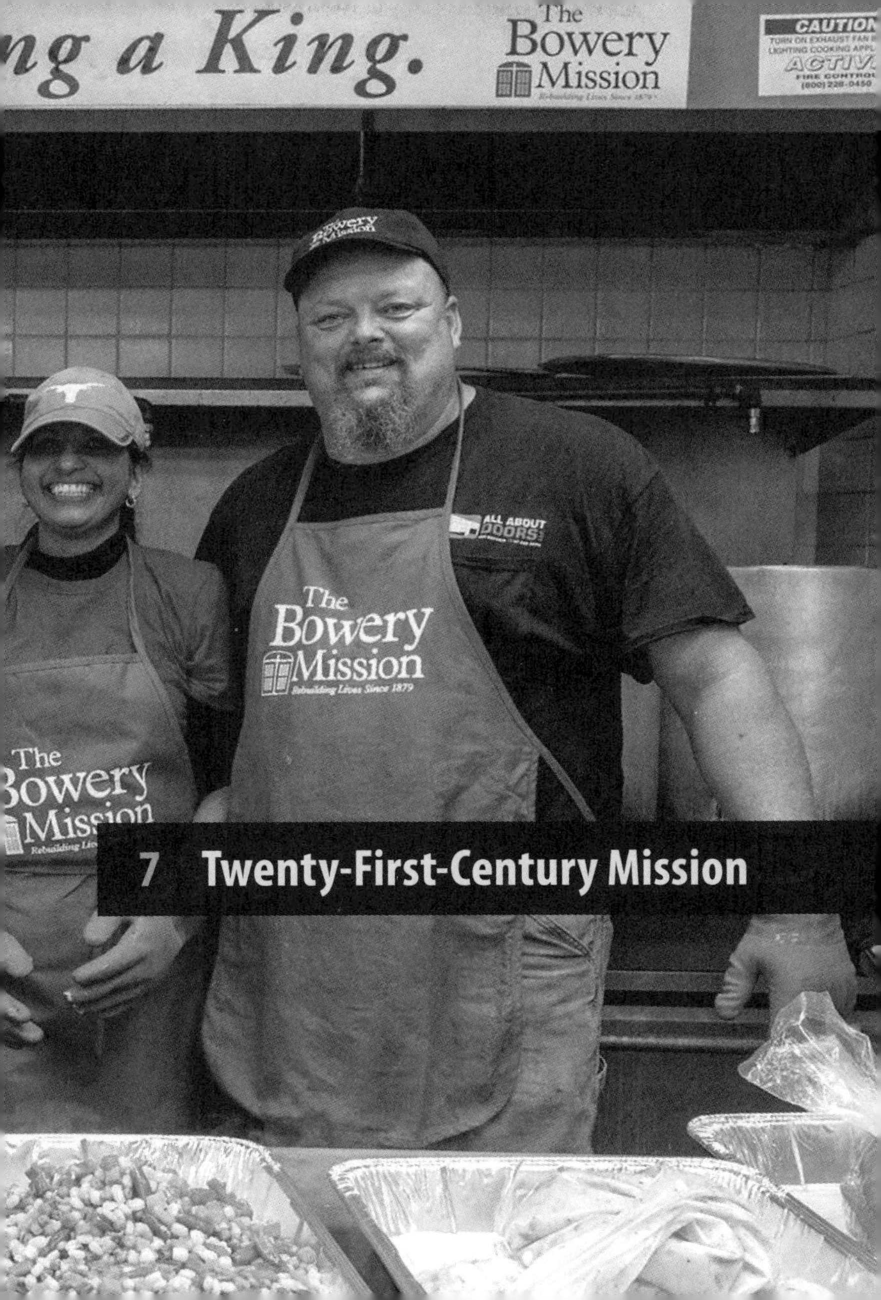

Robert "Slim" Perry had an impressive baritone voice. He sounded like a prophet when expounding scripture. Yet for over a decade he was chronically homeless, a regular at the Mission. The first time I saw him, he was lying outside an apartment building, semiconscious. Tenants were peering at him apprehensively, so I roused Slim and walked to the chapel with him. I got to know him well over the following months and years.

Slim told me that when he was eighteen, he returned from school one day to learn that his mother had just been raped by the neighborhood grocer. Slim knew where the family gun was kept and where to find the man. Grabbing the revolver, he dashed out and shot him. Slim was arrested, convicted of murder, and sentenced to eighteen years. When he left prison, having served the full term, he hit the bottle and the streets.

In 2014, Slim joined a project I initiated at the Mission. I gave participants disposable cameras and asked them to photograph their world. Slim became deeply involved, but sadly never saw the exhibition.

Slim mostly stayed sober at this time. On the Monday before Thanksgiving, however, I met him on the corner of Bowery and Rivington with a tall King Cobra in his hand. "Brother," I challenged, "you need to stop bowing to King Cobra, and give your life to King Jesus!" He threw his can to the curb, and we prayed together.

Slim was not drunk that night. He was merely heading for some place to sleep, most likely the apartment entrance where I had met him years before; the tenants had gotten used to him sleeping there. As he crossed the street, a speeding BMW hit him. He was killed on impact.

The other photographers decided to dedicate the show to his memory. Each had dictated a brief artist statement about their presentation. Slim's read:

> I want people to hear my story, hear my cry, but you're not going to see my tears. I'm homeless and an ex-convict, but at the same time, in all due respect, society has to reach out and help us. I need a job and housing. Don't just ignore us. We are looked at like dirt, but we are somebody.

It was a privilege for me to curate the project that meant so much to Slim. I dubbed it *Through My Lens: A Photographic Survey from Society's Margins*. The idea came from Augusto Boal's book *Theater of the Oppressed*, in which he describes a teacher in the slums of Lima, Peru, who asked his students to answer the question, "Where do you live?" by taking photos. The concept seemed simple enough to develop in our situation. Several clients enthusiastically joined in, transformed into artists or documentary journalists – whatever identity they chose. When they returned the cameras, to give them creative control I invited them to crop images or alter contrast and color. They then took me through each scene, telling its story as I recorded their words.

Too often, society stigmatizes the homeless or views them as passive objects of charity. *Through My Lens* affirmed their dignity, empowering all who took part. As artists and reporters, they knew they were contributing to the city's records and culture. The culmination came when *Through My Lens* photos were displayed beside established works of art at New Museum, at Ngam Restaurant in Soho, in James Chapel at Union Theological Seminary, and in the Mission's Fellowship Hall.

The pictures are intensely personal. One shot of a graffiti wall is titled "Mom," and its caption reads, "This reminds me of my mom – the lady leg and the big splotch over the rest of her. She left me when I was two." Other photos document the difficulty of finding a sleeping place, explore how the effects of childhood trauma linger throughout a life, or show evidence of compassion and friendship on the street.

Through My Lens stirred viewers to care about the photographers and their subjects. It received extensive coverage – from local blogs to magazines in China, Greece, Thailand, and Germany – and prompted similar shows in Boston and Texas.

New Museum and the International Center for Photography both partner with us to offer art programs. Yes, artistic expression has become intrinsic to the Bowery Mission, where a positive outlook is essential for staff and guests alike. I have seen those on society's margins find peace, even healing, through the arts. Since the Bible states, "In the beginning God created . . .,"[1] and its first chapter says we were made in God's image, I believe we were designed to be creative.

Augusto Boal's *Theater of the Oppressed* sparked yet another idea. Once a month, for a couple of years, Jeremiah Kyle Drake of Riverside Church came to the Mission and invited our guests to recreate injustices – and explore responses – through participatory theater.

One participant described jumping a turnstile when he could not afford subway fare. Two police officers had accosted him, at which he had retorted that he was homeless, had lost his ID, and was late for a benefits appointment. Each time the incident was reenacted, the man responded more calmly. He even played the police role one time – which gave him an entirely new perspective.

Shortly after we completed our photography project, an artist named Allie Wilkinson curated an exhibit called *FACE New York.* She had introduced artists from around the world to eighteen individuals on the Bowery, hoping to build relationships through art. Her statement reads:

> Through generous sharing and the meticulous process of drawing, painting or sculpting the uniqueness of a face, each team of subject and artist invites viewers to face the much more complex reality: that for each of the more than 60,000 people dealing with homelessness in New York City there is a different story, and a different face.

New York City remains fluid, as developers, politicians, and new waves of immigrants keep remolding the landscape. Trends ebb and flow, new drug forms replace old ones, and social status shifts with the flow of currency.

Since the turn of the millennium, the Bowery, for so long the city's grittiest street, has become increasingly valuable real estate. A plethora of upscale art galleries, restaurants, and cafés have sprung into being where brothels, dive bars, and flophouses once flourished. The Mission is now sandwiched between two new establishments. When the Salvation Army relocated to Brooklyn, it was replaced by Ace Hotel's Sister City, with glassy rooftop and Mediterranean menus, where guests will spend no less than two hundred dollars per night for a bed. On our other side towers the sleek New Museum, dedicated to contemporary art.

Remnants of the old Bowery, such as Andrews House and a couple of "hotels," are few and far between. Where the Sunshine Hotel bedded about one hundred and eighty men, only a handful now occupy a second floor. One of its three buildings was replaced twice, first by the Bowery Diner – where a hamburger costs eighteen dollars, slightly less than Peter Minuitt paid for Manhattan Island – and more recently by La Gamele, a chic French restaurant catering to the tastes of European tourists.

Thanks to some of our new neighbors, our kitchen now sometimes prepares decadent dishes. "It's Still Soup, but the Mushrooms Are Shiitake,"[2] reads a telling *New York Times* headline. Mission meals were always hearty, and the coffee was always hot, but these days boutique restaurants donate fresh produce, artisan coffee roasters provide quality beans, and catering companies contribute Camembert cheese and other culinary delights. Whole Foods Market gives us sushi and sashimi. I think the Mission's early leaders would approve. They set the precedent of giving our guests the best – since what we do for them, we do for Christ.

Despite improvements at the Mission, gentrification of the city, and sweeping changes countrywide, our nation's income inequality stubbornly persists; in fact, the divide keeps widening. Poverty, unemployment, family breakup, addiction, and PTSD still drive men and women to the street. The current number of home-less New Yorkers was paralleled only during the Great

Depression. In 2019, the Department of Homeless
Services reported an average of forty thousand adults
and twenty thousand children sleeping in city shelters every night. No one knows the number sleeping on
heating grates or in subways and other public spaces, for
fear of being hurt or robbed in the shelters.

Yes, here, where a pair of sneakers can sell for one
thousand dollars, we still serve about a thousand
free meals per day, and the destitute still flock to the
Mission's red doors in search of a second (or third, or
tenth) chance at life. One recent Thanksgiving, I watched
two lines forming on our block: New Museum patrons in
designer wear queued in one direction, to glimpse Lady
Gaga, while homeless folk lined up the other way for our
coat drive. One street, two worlds.

Emergency support is all some of our guests require.
Using our dormitories for a few weeks – or our Code
Blue Shelter in winter, when the chapel and Fellowship Hall remain open for sleep – may win them
time to get back into a spouse's good graces or save a
couple paychecks for rent. But the need is usually more
complex. Most folk on the street, in the throes of addiction or the aftermath of trauma, need far more than
short-term shelter.

Will the Bowery Mission solve the problem of homelessness in New York City? Probably not, but its partners
and staff, many of them formerly homeless themselves,

will continue to do their utmost. When Jesus told his disciples, "The poor you will always have with you,"[3] he wasn't making a cynical statement. He was quoting from Deuteronomy: "Since there will never cease to be some in need on the earth, I therefore command you, 'Open your hand to the poor and needy neighbor in your land.'"[4]

Wherever there is wealth, poverty is not far away. When the Bowery Mission first opened its doors, the dispossessed needed food, shelter, clothing, and work. A century and a half later, the needs are identical. And the Mission's message remains the same: God identifies with the poor, and we are all God's children. People who recognize this can claim a new identity – and begin to walk in dignity.

Timeline

1878:   Third Avenue elevated train (called the El) built

1878:   *Christian Herald* magazine founded in England by Joseph Spurgeon

1879:   Bowery Mission founded by Albert Ruliffson

1881–1895:   Bowery Mission superintendence of Josiah Ward Childs

1890s: Gilded Age

1891:   Hit song of 1891: "The Bowery" by Charles Hoyt

1893:   Financial panic

1894:   Founding of Mont Lawn Camp

1895:   Ruliffsons, Mission founders, depart New York City due to ill health

1895:   Henry Louis Klopsch becomes president of the Bowery Mission, organizes first board of directors. Christian Herald, owned by Klopsch, becomes corporate umbrella of Bowery Mission

1898:   Fire at Bowery Mission takes eleven lives

1899–1924:   Bowery Mission superintendence of John Hallimond

1899: Christian Herald publishes first Red-Letter Bible

1909: Dedication of chapel at 227 Bowery, attended by President Taft

1910: Klopsch dies

1910: J. C. Penney visits Bowery Mission after wife's death

1915: Fanny Crosby, Ellen Ruliffson, and Sarah Bird die

1925–1931: Bowery Mission superintendence of John R. Henry

1927–1966: Daniel Poling edits the *Christian Herald*

1929–1939: J. C. Penney supports Bowery Mission through Great Depression

1931–1941: Bowery Mission superintendence of Charles St. John

1939: Daniel Poling purchases the *Christian Herald*

1942: Bowery Mission superintendence of George Jacklin Kelly

1942–1959: Bowery Mission superintendence of George Bolton

1960s: Demographics of New York homeless begin to change. Irish, Italians, and Scandinavians are replaced by African Americans, Puerto Ricans, Caribbean Islanders, and non-European immigrants. There is a drastic increase in the number of mentally ill on the street. Heroin and other opioid addictions are on the rise.

1960–1966: Bowery Mission superintendence of Raymond J. Allen

1966–1968: Bowery Mission superintendence of Herbert Maynard

1969–1974: Bowery Mission superintendence of John Wilson Lockwood

1970s–1980s: Cocaine and crack become the prominent drug on the street

1974–1982: Bowery Mission superintendence of David G. Henritzy

1980: Bowery Mission acquires 229 Bowery and merges it into one building with 227

1984–1994: Bowery Mission superintendence of John Willock

1991: Christian Herald stops printing magazines, focuses on Bowery Mission work

1994: Edward Morgan becomes Christian Herald president

2015: David Jones becomes Christian Herald president

Acknowledgments

This book would not exist if it were not for the generations of ministers who have faithfully served New York City's poorest and most vulnerable through the Bowery Mission. These ministers are the unsung heroes who have served in the trenches, facilitating mealtimes, distributing clothes, breaking up fights, comforting the sick, and consoling those who have lost loved ones and those who have lost hope. There is not room to name them all, but these few represent the generations: Kimbell Frazer, Dady Johnson, Raffaelle DePalma, Gerald Manning, Basil Jones, Willie Dempsey, Spencer Gaynes, James Macklin, John DeSantos, Mary Bell, Vivian Hernandez, Carmella Hutson, Maria Velez, Sandra Mitchell-Morris, Kathy Kiesel, and Jo Clary.

Churches have always undergirded the work of these frontline ministers. The longest-standing church partnerships include Fifth Avenue Presbyterian; Calvary Baptist; Gospel Hall; the many Mennonite and Amish churches who lead services most weekends; George McCormack, who has led chapel services for more than fifty years; David Lee and Chinese Evangel Mission Church in Queens; Rex Duvall, who initiated the current form of the Bowery's Thanksgiving celebration in the 1980s; and Sharon Buntin and Abundant Life Church.

The Mission's work is further sustained by many partners, from Bombas, which regularly provides socks for our guests, to local coffee roasters who donate beans. I am immensely grateful for every donor, volunteer, and vocational partner – and for the countless other individuals and agencies who help the Mission meet the needs of the hurting and homeless. Of special note is the late Paul Beyers, who drove a tractor-trailer filled with food items from Pennsylvania to the Bowery every week for many decades, and Ms. Pauline Bethel, whose compassion for New York's suffering compelled her to move from rural Arkansas to Chinatown to serve regularly at the Mission.

My thanks to the current officers who steward the vision of the Bowery Mission – Dave Jones, James Winans, Craig Mayes, Cheryl Mitchell, Rob Depue, and Sarino Tropeano – and to the board of directors and friends of the Bowery, such as Nick Demarco, Dudley Diebold, Dan Houser, and Jan Nagel, who passed away during the writing of this book.

Thank you to Ed Morgan, who, when president at the Mission, always welcomed me into his office for conversation about the history and vision of this important work – an invitation that served as the seed of this book.

My personal gratitude to the Louisville Institute, and especially Don Richter and Keri Liechty, who have supported and encouraged me in a variety of ways over the years, in particular, by providing a grant to help sustain the research of this book. David Mulkins of the Bowery Alliance of Neighbors and Dr. Heather D. Curtis, associate professor of religion at Tufts University, have been invaluable resources.

I am thankful for the Plough team, especially my editors Helen Huleatt and Sam Hine, for their commitment to deeply investing in this book project.

To my advisors at Union Theological Seminary, Drs. John Thatamanil, Samuel Cruz, and Cornel West: thank you for affording me a rigorous education.

To those who struggle with housing insecurity, mental illness, substance abuse, personal and social trauma, and other forms of loss: you have shown me what it means to be part of the beloved community.

And to my faith community, the Manhattan Mennonite Fellowship: I am honored to serve as your pastor and thankful that you are my spiritual home.

Lastly, to my wife, Vonetta, and our children, Chloe and Elgin: your love has sustained me through seasons of flourishing as well as the most challenging seasons of ministry. May Christ always reign over our hearts and lives.

An Invitation

hope you have been inspired by these stories of the compassion and commitment of so many. Now that you've come this far, I invite you to take the next step and become a part of the Bowery Mission's present, as well as its future. For generations the Bowery Mission has brought together people from all walks of life to participate in God's miracle of life transformation. The Bowery Mission requires the talents, skills, and generosity of thousands of supporters to accomplish its daily goal of meeting the needs of New Yorkers without a home. I encourage you to learn more at *www.bowery.org*. If you find yourself in New York, please consider visiting or volunteering.

Each person experiencing homelessness is a beloved individual, holding untold promise and potential. Beneath the layers of poverty, shame, trauma, abuse, and desperation, that promise can be hard to see, and often even harder to uncover. With your help, the Bowery Mission will continue to uncover this potential in many even as we say "yes" to more people, more often, loving each person well. With your help, we will carry the Bowery Mission's legacy forward into a hopeful future.

Notes

1 Welcome to the Bowery

Photo: *Thanksgiving Dinner is served to the neediest at the Bowery Mission in NYC.* Photograph by Frances Roberts / Alamy.

1 "Oldest Street in Manhattan," Redeemer City to City (website), May 1, 2014.

2 "Foster Care Statistics 2016," Child Welfare Information Gateway (website), April 2018.

3 "Make Progress," The Bowery Mission (website).

2 Becoming Bowery

Photo: *The Bowery near Grand St., New York.* Library of Congress Prints and Photographs Division.

1 Horace Scandlin and Thomas Osborne, *The Wicked John Goode* (New York: Christian Herald, 1917), 87–88.

2 Scandlin and Osborne, 19.

3 Scandlin and Osborne, 102.

4 Scandlin and Osborne, 139–141.

5 Scandlin and Osborne, 139–141.

6 Theresa C. Noonan "The Bowery Mission," Landmarks Preservation Commission Report, June 26, 2012.

7 Elmer Bendiner, *The Bowery Man* (New York: Thomas Nelson, 1961), 42.

8 Noonan, "The Bowery Mission."

9 Elizabeth Blackmar, *Manhattan for Rent, 1785–1850* (Ithaca, New York: Cornell University Press, 1989).

10 "Did You Know This About the Bowery?" Bowery Alliance of Neighbors (website).

11 Joyce Mendelsohn, *The Lower East Side Remembered and Revisited* (New York: Lower East Side Press, 2001), 182.

12 Daniel B. Schneider, "F.Y.I.," *New York Times,* February 9, 1997.

13 John Frick, "Uncle Tom's Cabin on the Antebellum Stage," University of Virginia Institute for Advanced Technology in the Humanities (website).

14 Kelli Trapnell, "History of NYC Streets: Paradise Square," Untapped Cities (website), February 7, 2013.

15 "Bowery Slang," Bowery Boogie (website).

16 Walt Whitman, "The Old Bowery," in *Prose Works* (Philadelphia: David McKay, 1892).

17 Walt Whitman, "So Long," in *Leaves of Grass* (Ann Arbor: Lowe & B. Hould, 1855).

18 Bendiner, 55–56.

19 Mark Twain and Charles Dudley Warner, *The Gilded Age: A Tale of Today* (Hartford, CT: American Publishing Co., 1873).

20 Noonan, "The Bowery Mission."

21 Noonan, "The Bowery Mission."

22 "U.S. Immigrant Population and Share over Time, 1850–Present," Migration Policy Institute (website).

23 John Greener Hallimond, *The Miracle of Answered Prayer* (New York: Christian Herald, 1916), 72.

24 "Moody and Sankey Again," *New York Times,* October 1, 1879.

25 1 Cor. 1:27

26 Matt. 25:40

27 Owen Kildare, *My Old Bailiwick; Sketches from the Parish of "My Mamie Rose"* (New York: Fleming H. Revell, 1906).

28 Luc Sante, *Low Life: Lures and Snares of Old New York* (New York: Farrar, Straus & Giroux, 1991), 118.

29 Patrick R. Redmond, *The Irish and the Making of American Sport, 1835–1920* (Jefferson, NC: McFarland, 2014), 63.

30 "Eleven Killed in a Fire; Burned and Suffocated on the Upper Floors of the Bowery Mission Lodging House," *New York Times,* March 14, 1898.

31 "Eleven Killed in a Fire," *New York Times.*

32 "Manhattan Bridge Historical Overview," NYC Roads (website).

33 Noonan, "The Bowery Mission."

34 Julie Earle-Levine, "John Giorno's Half-Century on the Bowery," *T: The New York Times Style Magazine,* June 1, 2015.

35 Jack Kerouac, *Lonesome Traveler* (New York: McGraw-Hill, 1960).

36 "Dying Police Officer Kills Thug As 100 Cower in Bowery Mission," *New York Times,* January 9, 1960.

37 "Basic Facts About Homelessness: New York City," Coalition for the Homeless (website).

38 Brendan O'Flaherty, *The New Homelessness in North America: Histories of Four Cities,* Columbia University Department of Economics, November 1992.
39 Brendan O'Flaherty, *Making Room: The Economics of Homelessness* (Cambridge, MA: Harvard University Press, 1996), 46.

3 Magazine with a Mission

Photo: *Christian Herald cover, March 11, 1896.* Courtesy of the Bowery Mission.

1   Hallimond, 73.
2   Benedict Giamo, *On the Bowery: Confronting Homelessness in American Society* (Iowa City, IA: University of Iowa Press, 1989), 230.
3   Heather Curtis, *Holy Humanitarians: American Evangelicals and Global Aid* (Cambridge, MA: Harvard University Press, 2018), 257.
4   Robert M. Offord, *Jerry McAuley: His Life and Work* (New York: Ward & Drummond, 1885), 69–73.
5   Thomas De Witt Talmage, "Tenement Houses in NYC," *Christian Herald,* March 6, 1879; "The Poverty of the Very Poor," *Christian Herald,* November 14, 1878; "Night of Theft," *Christian Herald,* November 28, 1878.
6   Curtis, 11.
7   Noonan, "The Bowery Mission."
8   Norris A. Magnuson, *Salvation in the Slums: Evangelical Social Work, 1865–1920* (Metuchen, NJ: Scarecrow, 1977), 126.
9   Magnuson, 156.
10 Magnuson, 126.
11 "A Gentle Fundamentalist," *Time,* December 11, 1964.
12 Marvin Olasky, "The 'Gotcha' Clause," *World Magazine,* June 23, 2001.
13 The *Christian Herald*'s British edition ran from 1874 to 2006.
14 "Ed Morgan, Founder & Principal," Inspirational Leadership (website).

4 Bowery Mission Shapers

Photo: *Bowery Mission Breadline, 2:00 AM, 1906.* Lewis W. Hine.

1   John Hallimond and George Sandison, *Greatheart of the Bowery: Leaves from the Life-Story of John G. Hallimond* (New York: Fleming H. Revell Co., 1925), 12.
2   Obituary for John Hallimond, *New York Times,* November 22, 1924.
3   "New Year Welcomed," *New York Times,* January 1, 1900.

4   Magnuson, 50.

5   Hallimond, 81.

6   Hallimond, 82.

7   Hallimond, 15.

8   Hallimond, 15.

9   Hallimond, 81.

10 Hallimond, 81.

11 "New Year Welcomed," *New York Times.*

12 Hallimond, 102.

13 Hallimond, 103.

14 Hallimond, 16.

15 "Address on Missions; He Tells Methodists They are Forerunners of Civilization – Speaks at Bowery Mission," *New York Times,* December 14, 1909.

16 "Address on Missions," *New York Times.*

17 Roger A. Bruns, *The Damndest Radical: The Life and Work of Ben Reitman, Chicago's Celebrated Social Reformer, Hobo King, and Whorehouse Physician* (Urbana, IL: University of Illinois Press, 1986), 5.

18 "Mr. Martin Tells It All to the Bowery; Shaking Hands with the Unwashed After Laying Bare His Hopes for Humanity," *New York Times,* March 15, 1911.

19 "Franklin D. Roosevelt Speaks at Bowery Mission," *New York Times,* July 16, 1920.

20 "Mission Entertains 380; Music, Bread and Coffee Given to Bowery Refugees From Cold," *New York Times,* January 4, 1928.

21 Kildare, 180.

22 *Herald Democrat,* February 22, 1897.

23 Hallimond, 76.

24 Magnuson, 116.

25 Magnuson, 97.

26 Hallimond, 85.

27 Hallimond, 86.

28 Hallimond, 88.

29 In 1975, the organ was acquired by the United Methodist Church in Sudbury, Massachusetts, where it remains today.

30 Edith Blumhofer, *Her Heart Can See: The Life and Hymns of Fanny J. Crosby* (Grand Rapids: Eerdmans, 2005), 287.

31 Blumhofer, 327.

32 Blumhofer, 327.

33 Tony Carnes, "J. C. Penney, Jr, A Preacher's Kid," A Journey through New York City Religions (Website), August 22, 2016.

34 Tony Carnes, "J. C. Penney, Jr, A Preacher's Kid."

35 Charles Jackson St. John, *God on the Bowery* (New York: Fleming H. Revell, 1940), foreword.

36 St. John, 20.

37 St. John, 23.

38 St. John, 24.

39 St. John, 32.

40 St. John, 43.

41 St. John, 114.

42 "Milestones," *Time,* August 20, 1959.

43 Jane Margaret Laight, "George L. Bolton," IMDb (website).

44 "George Bolton, Bowery Pastor; Head of Christian Herald Mission Is Dead – Turned from Life of Gambling," *New York Times,* July 31, 1959.

45 Daniel Poling, "George Bolton Doesn't Preach to Empty Stomachs," *The Spartanburg Herald,* April 1, 1948.

46 Tony Carnes, *The Chapel: The Great Heart of the Bowery Mission* (New York: The Bowery Mission, 2009), 15.

47 "Overflow Crowds Hear Billy Sunday; Evangelist, Entering the Second Week of Revival, to Visit the Bowery Mission Tonight," *New York Times,* January 15, 1934.

48 Susan Orlean, *Saturday Night* (New York: Knopf, 1990).

5 Greatheart Chapel

Photo: *Singing Blessed Assurance in Chapel.* Courtesy of the Bowery Mission.

1 Noonan, "The Bowery Mission."

2 Noonan, "The Bowery Mission."

3 Noonan, "The Bowery Mission."

4 "Bowery Mission's New Home," *New York Times,* September 19, 1908.

5 Noonan, "The Bowery Mission."

6 "Dedicates His Boy to Aid Derelicts; Father Gives 'Jimmy' Hunt to Work of Saving 'Down-and-Outs,'" *New York Times,* November 9, 1913.

7 "Weds Her First Convert: Bowery Mission Worker Is Made a Bride at Hadley Rescue Hall," *New York Times*, December 26, 1911.

8 Murray Schumach, "A Wedding Is Held At Bowery Mission," *New York Times,* August 3, 1969.

9   Murray Schumach, "Bowery Worker Posed as Cleric; Ex-Alcoholic Says He Acted as Minister to Get Drinks," *New York Times,* August 9, 1969.

10 "I went from a teen pushing a cart to a man serving God," The Bowery Mission (website).

11 "Hallimond Funeral Puts Bowery in Tears; Throng Pay Last Tribute at Mission Which He Directed for 25 Years," *New York Times,* November 25, 1924.

6   On the Frontline

Photo: *Maundy Thursday footwashing.* Courtesy of the author.

1   Matthew 6:12
2   Ephesians 6:12
3   Matthew 25
4   St. John, 67.
5   Johann Christoph Arnold, *Cries from the Heart: Stories of Struggle and Hope* (Walden, NY: Plough Publishing House, 2014).
6   Proverbs 22:22
7   Luke 1
8   Jeremiah 20:14
9   Numbers 11:15
10 1 Kings 19:4
11 Amos 1:2
12 Genesis 16
13 Psalm 51:17
14 Jason Landsel, "Soldier of the Lamb," *Plough Quarterly* No. 2 (Winter 2015), 71–72.

7   Twenty-First-Century Mission

Photo: *Bowery Mission Thanksgiving.* Courtesy of the Bowery Mission.

1   Genesis 1:1
2   Julia Moskin, "It's Still Soup, but the Mushrooms are Shiitake," *New York Times,* July 2, 2003.
3   Matthew 26:11
4   Deuteronomy 15:11